Let Nothing Go To Waste

Cover Image: Elmira Railway Museum. Prince Edward Island. Dann Alexander

© **2020**
William Daniel Adams (Dann) Alexander
Frogsong Productions
ISBN 978-0-9881486-2-8

All rights reserved. No part of this publication may be reproduced or used or stored in any form or by any means – graphic, electronic or mechanical, including photocopying, or by any type of information storage or retrieval system without the prior written consent of the publisher. Absolutely any and all requests for photocopying, recording, taping or for information storage and retrieval system use, and for any classroom use shall be directed to the publisher or to Access Copyright, The Canadian Copyright Licensing Agency, whose contact information is kept up to date at www.AccessCopyright.ca

Also from the Author

Planned UnParenthood – Creating A Life Without Procreating.
ISBN 978-0-9881486-0-41

Throwing Dice
ISBN 978-0-9881486-1-1

Table of Contents

Title	Page
Disclaimer & Dedication	1
Radio Days Revisited	2
Truckin	15
Pathways and Walkways	19
When Wrestling Was Real	23
Junk Food Junking	28
You Want The Insurance?	34
Hitting The Hills	41
Live From The Basement!	47
Confirmation Classes	53
Mrs. Shopper	57
A Fast 3-Count	61
On The Eve of Examinations	63
Unfit Fitness and Basketball	73
Pizza Delivery	80
Jasper To Truro	83
Peace And Potatoes	96
No Thanks, Just Looking	103

Title	**Page**
CAUTION! Contains Language	107
Public Speaking (In Private)	110
Want To Drive?	116
Old Dust and Old Memories	119
Black & White Television Dinners.	122
Goal Thief	124
At The Movies	126
Green Grass	130
The Cable Is Out!	135
Well, That Was Stupid!	140
For Joe Fraser	148
Mowing With Scissors	152
Afterword	153

Disclaimer & Dedication

The following book contains words.

These are meant to provoke emotions.

By reading these words, you are accepting graciously the consequences of whatever happens next.

Hopefully, you will find entertainment within these pages.

This is dedicated to the memory of J. David Alexander, my Brother from the same Mother, and Father.

Radio Days Revisited

Music was always around. My earliest memories of musical sounds were Johnny Cash records on the turntable. The Tommy Hunter[1] Show was on CBC Television Saturday nights. With Hunter's famed variety show there was exposure to gospel-tinged music and some of the very early country music songs.

I was fortunate to have been drawn to radio at a young age. It was an escape and an education. The local a.m. station was what we heard mostly when radios were blaring. If no one liked the local station, they turned into the many Prince Edward Island channels we could easily get. There were many radios scattered throughout the whole house. The main radio was an old Sears home-stereo device which also contained an eight-track tape player. The turntable was hooked up to it for the constant spinning of records. Even when we did get cable

---

[1] I met Tommy Hunter when I was four. I would then later interview him for a Thunder Bay Newspaper article for his final tour.

television, the radio still played an important everyday role at home.

One of my many obsessions as a young bloke was reading astrological predictions in the newspaper. So when the local radio station started reading broadcasts of "the stars" in the mornings, it drew me closer to the speakers. For a time, I really believed the Aries forecast might dictate exactly how my day at school would go. It really was a way to set myself up for disappointment. The mentality would enter my head to watch for things that were predicted that morning on the radio. I really believed the nonsense.

Through the early years of my youth I started having to fall asleep to the radio sounds at night. Radio became a constant comfort. It was much easy to tune out the talking and just get into the music. There were occasions when I would tune in a baseball game from Boston or New York clear up the eastern seaboard. Sometimes that would happen late at night when I could not sleep. You really did feel like you could tell what was going on listening to those games. Calling sports for the radio sounds like a challenge compared to calling for television. In my view, the radio commentators really needed to paint bigger pictures to help with visualization. Television gives you a picture to follow along with. Radio is theater of the mind.

In the mid 1980's, I started to collect music for my own enjoyment. There were things I wanted to play on my own cassette player so I could listen to music in my room. One of the things I did was keep a blank tape on standby at all times. This was so I could capture an interesting song and eventually go get it if I could. It became fascinating to record the dialogue of the on-air personalities and how they would talk up a track[2]. The station ran a "Favourite 5" countdown during the weeknights. This was the equivalent of having an American Top 40 show during the week. Whoever was working the evening shift would take calls and record votes as to the favourite five songs of the day. More often than not it accurately might reflect the top songs on Billboard Music charts for the week. On the weekends I was a fan of Casey Kasem and Shadoe Stevens and listened to their respective Top 40 shows regularly.

Over a short time some of the local radio personalities knew me from my frequent call-in requests. They never hesitated to play and dedicate a song to a girl I had a longing for.

---

[2] Talking up a track is introducing a song as it starts or just before it starts. DJ's might improvise a story about the song or mention something in relation to it.

I was a silly kid. A dreamer, but a bit daft thinking those dedications would actually work. The local station eventually adopted an open dedication line. This is where they would pick a target song then take open calls on the air for people to promote a dedication. It was absolute chaos and mayhem from day one. In between one or two serious dedications was a flurry of fake ones and crank calls. In time I started to participate in the mischief. It was hilarious to the kids of the county. There was a collection of us who worked to start taping the dedication line. We were ready to catch a moment of comedy gold over the airwaves. The personality who regularly worked the evening show would usually get irritated within the first few bad calls. Sometimes he would join in the banter or exact his own revenge on a caller. I remember vividly one call where someone laid out a veiled death threat against a girl who was making a move on her man. Live and on the air, The DJ called her back.

"Hi, thanks for being an idiot, and have a nice day".

He had finally snapped! I doubt that the program directors would have taken any disciplinary action for his retaliation. They might have done the same thing. There was another occasion where this same radio host took a call from an angry lady who started to threaten her former friend live on the air. He calmly hung up, suggesting that everyone needs to "have a nice cup of decaff".

One of the best on-air calls that I remember was around the time when the story broke chronicling the arrest of Paul Reubens (Pee Wee Herman) for his alleged public display of exhibitionism in a movie theater. A local genius phoned the dedication line to dedicate the target song to "Pee Wee Herman, from his hands". The DJ completely lost his composure. He was laughing for a good minute before moving on to the next call.

In 1999 when I moved to Canmore Alberta I received my first taste of what classic rock radio sounded like. By this time I had become more critical of popular radio because it was all music that my ears could barely tolerate. A real classic rock format was something I never heard. Its' existence was out there, but you don't think of it as being a real possibility until you actually hear it. Calgary's Rock 97 was just getting underway with a killer format of classics. Hearing this format was such a breath of fresh rocky mountain air. When classic rock aired on the old hometown station, it was only very late at night. Even then it would be only a song or two.

I became an instant fan of this station. I was driving a 1988 Camaro with a factory stereo always set to the station. There were a few tapes kicking around at any time throughout the front seats for me to crank out some other stuff when I wanted to switch off the station.

In time due to my phone calls and faxed requests, I started to get to know some of their on air talent. The core group was a talented bunch who kept many people tuned in. A great benefit to becoming a regular caller was my increased chances of winning prizes. Luckily, there were a few times I would manage to win a few things while listening to Rock 97. There was a t-shirt and temporary tattoos that I once wore to a concert featuring The Guess Who and Joe Cocker.

The station hosted a CD listening party for Rush's much anticipated[3] "Vapor Trails" album. The location was a popular Irish Pub in downtown Calgary. I remember briefly rapping with one of the morning drive hosts as he sipped a cold Guinness. My company that night was a friend who knew little of Rush but as the night went on started to try and understand it a bit. The station gave me a copy of one of their classic albums which I would then give to her.

One of the other personalities who worked as a floater covering different shifts threw a

---

[3] Anticipated by only Rush fans I suspect.

Rush t-shirt at me which was a really cool moment. With Rush being one of my favourite bands there was never a t-shirt in my collection from them. It would be one that I would wear out completely. It was a black shirt that faded to light gray before coming apart at the sleeves.

The chap who gave me that shirt would later flip me a couple of tickets to a show by Scottish rock and roll legends Nazareth. There was not even a contest running when I called in. I called to phone in a track to be played since I was going to be hanging out in the back warehouse at my place of employment for the afternoon.

"Call me back in a few minutes". He interjected before I could even get word of the song request.

"I'll hook you up with something. (click)."

The something turned out to be tickets to this show. The tickets represented the first actual date my spouse and I went on. She's probably even more of a Nazareth fan than I ever would be. She knows songs of theirs that are still unfamiliar to me. We have a copy of their greatest hits record on vinyl. We could easily hear any of the songs during the day on radio because the band remains a perennial favourite for rock radio disc jockeys.

One evening while lounging in the cool upstairs of my Calgary apartment, the lady who I would eventually marry called me with a sad tone to her voice.

"Turn on the radio".

A flick of the switch to Rock 97 revealed no Rock on the 97. It was hip-hop[4].

"What?"...

We were dumbfounded. It was difficult at the time to understand how a station that was so popular could just flip formats so suddenly.

The following Monday I joined a chorus of regular listeners calling the station headquarters to express my dissent with the format change. We flooded the voice mails and kept the phones ringing for days.

A few days later I thought a visual statement could be made. The radio station broadcasted from a location close to my workplace. One of the popular items my work carried was an aerosol spray chalk can which washed away once a surface was hosed down or rained on. After checking in to the desk for the work day and with permission from my supervisor, I drove up to the station with my now-tattered Rock 97 shirt in tow. After pulling into the vacant parking lot, I laid the shirt down in the walkway leading to the front entrance. I

---

[4] I'm a fan of old-school hip-hop, very little of the modern era.

traced the outline of the shirt in hot pink aerosol chalk, left it there and drove away.

I'm sure it did nothing but make people think the person who did this was insane. I saw it as a form of unique protest.

Interestingly enough, the new hip-hop format did not last long. The station would flip to the new to Canada format of JACK FM. The format has since gone on to become one of the most successful in radio history. It was a mix of adult-oriented rock with classics and modern music.[5]

Through JACK FM I spent part of a memorable morning working a great bit with the morning drive co-hosts. This was in order to win tickets to a performance from one of my comedy heroes. Eric Idle of Monty Python's Flying Circus[6] was coming through town as part of "The Greedy Bastard Tour". I had an idea to call the station and sing songs from the Monty Python shows and movies for as long as they wanted in order for me to win tickets. The morning co-hosts at the time were Matt O'Neill[7] and Eric Francis. Matt has become a radio legend in his own right

---

[5] The JACK FM format originated as an American internet radio stream. Rogers Communications eventually moved many stations to this format in 2002.
[6] If you do not know who they are, we cannot be friends.
[7] Matt is the chap who was sipping a Guinness at the Rush Vapor Trails CD release party.

while Eric is more famously known now for his work as a hockey commentator. When I pitched the idea to them on singing the songs for a period, they agreed right away and we worked it in as a bit. For about an hour I had to make it seem like I was singing any song I could think of from the Pythons. When they would go to a break or a song they would flip to the line I was on and tell me to take a break. One of them would flip back on and tell me to start singing again so when they were on the air, they would "check" to see if I was still singing.

I won the tickets and they were well worth it. Eric Idle put on a memorable show consisting of classic sketches and new material. He mentioned he was writing a musical to be called Spamalot. I thought he was joking. Fourteen Tony Award nominations with three wins later, I know he most certainly was not kidding.

Many of the radio voices from Calgary that I had the pleasure of getting to know are still in the business. Samantha Stevens to me is the Queen of Canadian radio. It is important that I mention her and Deanna Nason in this chapter. I am thankful to them for their kindness over the years.

Every few years I end up re-connecting with one of the chaps who worked evenings at my hometown station. He is long out of the radio business but always showed great patience with me and the other radio nerds who called the station nightly attempting to get our songs and comments on the air. He long moved on to much better paying work. You could not blame him for it. Through him and others I learned that going into radio might not be the best idea. The pay is low in many markets and you end up having to move everywhere just to get good paying work. I had a difficult time imagining the possibility of working somewhere playing stupid music for a stupid paycheck just to be in the business. One of the people I knew in the business was working a second job at an Ontario Beer Store. He has been one of the lucky ones, having now moved into journalism on a full-time basis.

Radio has seen many changes. Anyone with a Smartphone can access an endless supply of radio streaming apps and podcasts. Some decry the move away from strong local voices on every radio dial.

Satellite radio appears to be losing steam to podcasting. Satellite still has a loyal audience and provides music formats listeners would not always hear on the traditional terrestrial radio airwaves. Music has to have its' traditional vehicle in order for it to reach the masses.

Choice was something we did not have back in the younger days. Now the choices are endless. Today anyone willing to put in the work can start a podcast. Some of those podcasts have gone on to become major successes. Advertisers have another medium to sell products and services.

One of the great things satellite and podcasting has done is educate listeners on the history of broadcasting.

In my opinion, many of the Jack Benny radio programs are still fresh sounding today as they were back when they first aired. Satellite and podcast platforms continue to grace listeners with radio classics such as George Burns and Gracie Allen, Dragnet, Gunsmoke and many others. Classic radio offers teachable moments to artists studying writing and dialogue. Delivery is something, timing is everything.

A few summers back, there was a glimmer of hope from a straight-talking disc jockey in northeastern Nova Scotia when working a weather forecast. We were bracing for a hellish heat wave with temperatures set to soar into the high thirties.[8] In describing the pending scorcher, he simply commented;

"The heatwave is coming for us all, and we're all gonna die".

---

[8] Celsius

Without skipping a beat he went straight into a song.[9] I remember laughing hysterically thinking that there was hope for the newer generations of on-air personalities.

---

[9] Song = Record. The correct term is straight into a record.

Truckin

It was a combination of light cool and navy blue. One of the many Chevrolet S-10 trucks that was commonly seen on the roads in the nineteen-eighties and early nineties. A truck that stood a chance of lasting longer than the first one Dad owned. That one was an ugly faded orange crush Datsun, ready to blow apart at the bolts.

A few days after driving the S-10 home, Dad discovered pinhole leaks in the gas tank that never ended up getting fixed. A few weeks after the purchase, it needed major repair work. Once that repair work was completed, it never needed another stitch of work and was literally driven into the ground, still full of pinhole leaks in the fuel tank. He drove a few of its' final years without any insurance. It was being driven the five minute drive from home to the power plant where he worked. Once I obtained my license he put insurance back on it again. By this point there were too many close calls where a bored police officer might have pulled him over for speeding or forgetting his seatbelt.

I frequently rode in the bucket fold down seats on trips into town. Not the most comfortable things to be sitting on. A sudden stop would have you slingshot sideways.

One year Dad received a collection of tapes of Gordon Lightfoot music as a gift. These all ended up in the truck. You knew that if radio was not happening then you would be listening to Lightfoot. One of my best mates to this day will mention listening to Lightfoot in the truck. It was part of the many lessons I would learn on music and words. Lightfoot's music is very much a part of who I am. Many of my positive memories of the old man are because of this music and the old truck.

One weekend the old man and I did a short road trip out to a golf course along the Northumberland Shore. Brule Point offered a break from where we all usually hit golf balls in nearby Pictou. The drive takes you out through some pristine cottage country and coastal communities. The roads are winding and worn. We were taking our time in the old truck and contemplating a lunch stop along the way. For several minutes a woman and her young child were driving close behind. You could see them so clearly, you would have thought they were sitting in the bucket seats of our truck. After several minutes Dad grew annoyed and pulled over to wave them ahead. He was driving the speed limit. The woman sped up, rapidly vanishing from site. Not less than a minute later, we rounded a corner to find the woman's car pulled over in front of a police cruiser with lights blaring. The police had nabbed her for speeding.

The old man and I pointed and laughed at her as we slowly drove by. Justice rightfully served.

One other memory with that truck was one night I remember visiting him at his then girlfriend's place. She had an apartment a few streets over from where my Mom and I lived. On that night when visiting, there was a pouring rainstorm and he still had a few things to do before going home for the evening. I cannot remember exactly what is all was that needed to be done. He was not planning to stay long. It was pouring rain outside. He wanted some gas put in the tank before he started the drive to his home so he could save a few minutes in the morning. At this point I had my license only a short time so I was just happy to have the truck out for a spin. The rain sheets slammed into the windshield, splashing out and away from my field of vision. Wipers swept furiously at the glass with little avail. That was one of the last times I ever drove the old thing. It was just a cool rainy night for a late night drive.

The old man held on to that truck until it literally started to burst apart. Before he eventually had it towed away for scrap, I made a plea with him to sell it to me for a bargain. I knew someone who could hook me up with a gas tank from a salvage yard. Someone I knew could have put it on properly. Long gone would have been the pinhole leaks in the tank. It needed a new battery just to get it going again. It was advertised from $650.00 for a few weeks, then down to $450.00. Eventually it went for whatever the old man could get.

It probably needed to go and I was in denial over it. Dad never talked about getting another truck. He never did. Then again, he also swore one day he would never buy a new vehicle.

Then one day, he did just that. He bought an ugly blue Ford Focus Station wagon.

I miss that truck.

Pathways and Walkways

It was my early teens when my parents divorced. Mom moved into an apartment on the west-side of New Glasgow. The idea of being closer to things after years of living in the country was alluring to me. A person didn't always have to drive to get somewhere.

A supermarket was a few blocks away. You could easily carry four or five bags of groceries all the way back to the apartment. A friend had introduced me to some of the shortcut pathways around town. Two of the pathways still stand out to me. One started at the end of a section of town where older-style homes sat with large yards. Once you went through a place I could only describe as a valley in the woods, you came out the other end close to a section of Munroe Avenue.

The other memorable pathway was at the very top of Munroe Avenue. The best way to describe Munroe is to think of it as busy long stretch of hill. It would make for a great daily cardio workout.[10] At the very top of it is where a water reservoir tower stands. A path through the trees starting at the tower led out to the Highland Square Mall. The mall was a place I frequented as a mall rat on many weekend nights. I spent countless hours in the arcade coughing up quarters into the many machines. Between developing my arcade and pinball skills, there would be an occasional break to grab a soft drink. Lapping that mall probably kept us in good shape. If Fitbits had been around at the time, I'm certain I would have clocked several kilometers just in mall walks. Good practice for when I turn 94 I suppose.

In walking around town, sticking to the main roads of was smart from a safety perspective. One would be less likely to get jumped at night by a carload of idiots chancing an assault charge. Even into the early hours of the morning, most of New Glasgow was lit well enough that if something unusual was happening, someone could possibly end up witnessing something.

The late evening walks were the most memorable and the most calming. If there was a moment where I needed some peace

---

[10] A former friend lived at the top of Munroe Avenue for much of his life. He walked over to school and home for lunch every single day. This is no short walk for a small town.

and quiet before crashing out, I would walk a few blocks with music turned up in my headphones. As someone who found sleeping difficult to begin with, there were a few nights that walking did help. Living a life completely caffeinated up on boatloads of colas did nothing to improve my health and sleep. It just kept me wired for what felt like days on end. When the big name brand cola was not on sale, we were content to settle for the store brand equivalent. I developed an addiction to the food safe version of speed.[11]

When I moved to Canmore, Alberta in 1999, walking became a regular thing again. Canmore's main areas of business were an easy stroll. Locals schooled me early in staying tuned in to warnings of cougars[12] and bears. Streets had "bear proof" dumpster bins for garbage. There were ample stories of people losing their pets to the hungry wildlife. The reality was that developers were continuing to encroach on their territory. So wildlife started to come closer to town out of a sense of survival.

On my move into Calgary, there was a time when walking was part of my peace even though I had owned a vehicle for some time.

---

[11] Caffeine.
[12] Also known as mountain lions to some.

One of the communities I lived in was home to a very interesting upscale retail area. A high-end grocery store, along with a coffee shop, book store and clothing boutique made the pedestrian traffic an interesting watch. There were multiple Saturdays when I would just start walking or running in the direction of Calgary's downtown core. The first time doing this journey led me to a great pathway that brought me alongside Calgary's Elbow River. Perfect warm spring weather, the green already showing strong in the grass, water calmly moving along, it was its' own kind of peace.

In all the places I have lived, I can connect hikes, strolls and runs to good memories.

When Wrestling Was Real

It was a con job I completely fell for. The violence, the storylines, we believed it and bought into it. We thought that people who worked the inside of a wrestling ring were legitimately fighting. A few grownups kept telling us goofy kids that it was staged. We didn't believe it and never wanted to. My grandfather knew it was staged and still found entertainment value in it when we went to matches during the summer at the old New Glasgow Stadium.

Saturdays meant that wrestling would be on television. The sport was reaching such a crescendo during this period in the 1980's that it was on television multiple times during a weekend. For a couple of years, my brother and many of our friends never missed it. We wanted someone to cheer for. When the New Brunswick based promotion of Atlantic Grand Prix Wrestling aired later in the day we all tuned in as part of the large television-viewing audience. During the summer months the promotion went on the road with a great roster of performers. There would often be multiple shows happening on the same day in different places. Sunday night was the night for New Glasgow. They had no problems getting good numbers on the gate.[13] The draws were always solid and the performers and promoters made money. A two hour card was easy to fill and fun to watch. Dad was never really a fan but saw how much we all enjoyed it. My grandfather would be in it with us hollering towards the ring area. His thick Scottish accent would cut through the smoke and sounds in the small arena. Any of the bad guy heels that drew heat were surely to get an earful from the loud Scotsman in the stands.

The promotion would sell photographic prints of the bigger stars of the business who didn't even work with Atlantic Grand Prix at the time. I would find out later that some of the people in the pics actually did come to our part of the world earlier in their careers. They must have secured a deal with the larger promotion to allow for prints to be sold. The companies that employed those bigger names in wrestling made money no matter what was attached to them.

We ended up taping many of those pictures in our bedrooms. Only one time I obtained an autograph at a local event. Midway through a card I spotted the

---

[13] The "gate" is the sum of money taken in from ticket sales.

legendary performer who wrestled as The Great Malumba. He was a treasured fan favourite who always knew how to get audiences going. He was a real entertainer. He was leaning against the arena glass dressed in street clothes watching intently during an ongoing match involving another fan favourite, Ruben Cruz. Cruz was a popular Puerto Rican performer. He won himself a large fan base wrestling in Canada between Calgary's Stampede Wrestling, and Atlantic Grand Prix Wrestling working under the name Hercules Ayala Cortez. The ongoing match had some kind of no-disqualification setup. This is a way for the promoter to work in an illusion of potential for violence outside the wrestling ring. During the match, I approached Malumba to have him autograph my picture. He politely waved me off, saying "later, later".

I was smart enough to sense that something was going on and maybe he was there for a purpose given his intense concentration on the match. Sure enough, as the in-ring action spilled out to the arena floor and then a separate stage area, Malumba interfered to save Hercules Ayala from a "beating". Ayala scored the pinfall right outside the rink glass door where Malumba was hanging out. He was waiting for a queue from the booker[14] to step in as part of the show. At the time, it all seemed very real.

One of those nights, an audience member did take things too far and almost ended up beaten for real. "Bulldog" Bob Brown was a large bloke who spent plenty of time working in Canada. Between Calgary and Atlantic Canada, he was a well-known name and a well-hated heel.[15] Brown also had a successful career working in America. He was drawing heat from someone in the near front-row at ringside. He was someone from town so I have serious doubts that he was a mark[16] put there by the booker to get something else going. Some words were exchanged and Bulldog Brown walked up and spit on the guy. As the audience member was about to charge Brown, several people nearby stood up to hold him back.

It was only a couple of years later that I figured out the reality of professional wrestling. After that I might occasionally check in on the news of what was happening but I pretty much stopped watching it immediately. Every once in a while though I

---

[14] Person who determines outcome of wrestling matches.
[15] "Bad guy" or rule breaker in wrestling.
[16] Person planted in the audience by the booker to interact with performers and add element of drama to matches.

will drift on to YouTube and pull up a classic clip from the Atlantic Grand Prix days. It's fun to see an old-school show. Wrestling was once an entertaining spectacle where the focus was on the athleticism. It really gave the illusion of violence happening in front of you. Wrestling was simple back then. You cheered for the good guys and hurled verbal jabs at the bad guys. That straight-forward simplicity is long gone. It's no longer entertaining or worth watching.

It was better when we all thought it was real.

Junk Food Junking

I was a so-called "picky" eater. My parents both grew up eating bland food with little variety on the plates. Dad grew up with boiled vegetables as a side dish for almost everything. His Mom was Prince Edward Island born and raised, growing up with fresh vegetables throughout the summer and fall. The three spices they all knew were salt, pepper, and extra salt. Let's be real. From a health perspective boiled vegetables were still better than no vegetables. My Dad and Grandfather were both Scotsmen, one a little brasher than the other. Grandfather "Jocko" knew of only the exact same spices as my Grandmother. No wonder they were married for over sixty years.[17]

However, I loved spending lunch times in Jocko and Gran's dining room. I've enjoyed more meals there than I can ever recall. Where Gran shone brightly with spices was in her baking abilities. There were always fresh sweets around. She loved all of them.

---

[17] Mutual spice admiration was not an actual factor to their lasting marriage.

There were cookies and cakes and other things with cinnamon, allspice, nutmeg and who the hell knows what else. Eating sugary sweets would take a toll on her health. Surprisingly, she managed to live into her eighties with diabetes. I'm glad she was around for as long as she was.

Let me return back to the boiled vegetables. Every night at the dinner table as a kid was a fight. I thought most vegetables were disgusting. I was happy with fries. My favourite lunches were grilled cheese and fries. They were among the first things I learned to prep on my own. Occasionally, the smoke detectors would go off while the bread slices crisped to a fine coat of glossy black. This was the result of carelessly forgetting the stove was on while working on the latest video-game conquest.

After my parents separated, each of them had some very different foods in their respective fridges and cupboards. My cola addiction had long set in and I waited anxiously for Pepsi or Coke to go on sale. In time, I settled for whatever store-made brand was available at respective supermarkets. We never drank water unless it was part of our tea and coffee. Dad regularly stocked up on 24-packs of store-brand cola from the local co-op market. We never ran out of the stuff at his place. To her credit, Mom tried her best to keep it out of her fridge. It never worked well given that she regularly sent me for groceries. It was handy having a store a short walk down the street from her apartment. "I don't know how that bottle of Pepsi got there!"

If I arrived home to her place with a bottle of Pepsi or Coke, she understandably would get irritated. That fire was flamed by my ability to "accidentally" add 4-packs of Eat-More bars along with several bags of chips into the carts. Junk food was truly an escape for me. Here I was never gaining a single pound eating garbage food. I felt invincible with a turbo-charged metabolism. Not once did I think this kind of eating and ignorance would catch up to me or show up in other ways. It would be a few years before I arrived at destination healthy reality. Even with that present reality, I am fully aware my days of poor eating could still catch up to me.

For whatever reason, a salad was almost viewed as a fancy luxury in the old household. This is idiotic when you consider vegetables are not that expensive in most of Canada.[18] Dad's idea of a salad was a very basic set of ingredients.

---

[18] Except for the three territories, where fresh produce comes at a premium due to high cost of transport. Even though it is partially subsidized! The vegans and vegetarians in the territories make due with frozen and canned products.

1. Iceberg Lettuce.
2. Field Cucumber
3. Slices of firm tomato.
That was it.

I never knew what a caesar salad was until my early teens. Even then I don't think I actually ate one until moving to Alberta. When I moved out west, one of my favourite foods to order was a gourmet caesar salad from a nearby eatery. I was boarding in a house with a family I had just met. So, I was nervous to join them in mealtimes at first. For those first few weeks, I spent a great deal of time between this eatery eating salads and at a nearby pub ordering fish and chips. That pub was pure peace to be in even on a noisy evening. Locals' night was $2.50 a beer. Those were glorious times in a beautiful mountain town, getting drunk for the sacrifice of a twenty-dollar bill.

The family I was boarding with opened my eyes to more food. The matriarch of the home became a second mom to me and knew right away I had issues with food. When she and others in the house put on a big meal, they put out multiple kinds of salads. I took to sampling all of them. The horizons expanded. Still the junk food remained. I developed a further weakness for gourmet pastries, cookies and cakes that I didn't know even existed.

It wasn't until my thirties where I took notice of how difficult my eating was from a health perspective. I started to read more. Through my spouse, my learning increased because she read more health content. She wanted to take charge of her health so it was going to inspire me to do the same thing. It had to be a team effort. We needed to help each other out.

September of 2017 was an awakening. After many years of preaching animal rescue and animal rights, it was time for a change. It was time to start practicing what I preach. Many people who embrace veganism know this feeling. They suddenly make the connection. It's an overwhelming feeling that is difficult to describe. I went through a period of grief and sorrow lasting several days. How could I do this? How can I preach a gospel of compassion while shoveling my face full of animals? I knew fully what was happening. It was not oblivious to me how the food supply chain worked. It's difficult to pretend reality doesn't exist when reality is proven real. A dog's life is just as important as a cow being hauled to slaughter. I have significant problems communicating with farmers who claim to raise their herds "with love", knowing what happens to them next.

There are things I have seen that may never get out of my mind. It's hard to understand right now how anyone who has embraced veganism can go back to eating animal products. Knowing the ethical, health and environmental consequences now, I am grateful to be where I am with food. Sure I still take part in some rare moments of junk food junkin.

Only now it's vegan junk food. Even those moments are few. I've been told by multiple physicians including my own, that whole plant food eating is the best thing a person can do.

You Want The Insurance?

In the early 2000's, Alberta was never short of work for someone determined to find it. Few places were accepting resumes by email at this stage of the digital revolution. You still needed to knock on doors, send a few faxes or even gamble some stamps and throw some in the mail.

One of the emails I sent made it through to one of the major car rental companies. For the story I'll refer to it as "Stellar Car". Somewhere in the middle of a long evening of music and junk food, I applied to the "management training program" of this particular company.

Let me explain something before I continue. During the latter part of the 1990's and early 2000's several of the major players in the vehicle rental business advertised for "Management Trainees". It was a smart way to draw in resumes from young eager professionals looking to make a living. It gave off the impression that you could quickly rise to the top! One particular company still advertises job postings today asking people if they want to join their management trainee program. You can make it to the top!

What did the top mean? Would you graduate from renting cargo vans to renting Ferraris? I didn't really care at this point.

There were some really good people working the rental counter desks. Rarely was anyone mean or ignorant. The ignorant we had to fear were the customers who expected royal treatment when they sure as hell didn't deserve it. The job was a base salary plus commission. If you don't know anything about the rental vehicle business, let me explain how the bonuses are earned.

Many drivers now have a rider on their vehicle insurance that will cover them if they should suffer an incident while driving the rental car. Many credit card companies offer car rental insurance as a bonus incentive for having the card. If a person does not have insurance, the requirement is to purchase coverage offered by the rental agency. Where I worked, the basic daily rental insurance coverage was $15.99 per day. In addition to the basic coverage, a more comprehensive package of around $5.99 per day was offered. It would provide a person with a reduced deductible in the event of an accident, to cover for emergency necessities and a few other things. That extra insurance was where we would earn some bonus cash. Keep in mind the majority of renters never have to make a claim against the coverage they purchase. So the companies make an extra profit by selling this coverage. Some of that goes to the rental agent in the form of commission.

I remember a chap called Ed who frequently sold the extra insurance packages to willing customers. One morning there was a group of customers from Asia, in to rent two mini-vans for their groups. There were about six in each group and all were to be put as drivers on each of the vehicles. Somehow Ed sensed they had money to spend. He alerted me to them so I could watch what he was about to do.

Within a half-hour, Ed earned a large slice of commission towards his next payday. It was not because of any language difficulty. The tourists' English was perfect. Ed had sold them on a "gold" level assistance package that didn't even exist. For $8.99 _per day_, _per driver_, they would have a zero deductible to pay should something happen to the vehicles they were driving. No accidents happened. Safe to assume they had a great journey. Ed enjoyed a larger paycheck on that pairing of contracts alone.

One morning during my short career as a car rental agent, we were told a training session was being held at a nearby hotel conference center. A trainer from head office in Toronto was coming out for the weekend to work a few shifts and give a presentation on sales. I'll call him Enthusiastic Brent. While I appreciated Brent's passion, it bordered on ridiculous. He told his story about starting as a counter rep and quickly worked his way up to a position as a corporate trainer. He talked about how sometimes he came to work on a Saturday because he truly loved what he did. He admitted he was not getting paid for those Saturdays.

He admitted working for free.[19]

Free for a car rental agency. That did it. He was officially a loony in my books. Looking back I cannot fault him for his passion. Part of his training was something that would stick with me for a few jobs after this one. He insisted we should answer the phone "It's a great day at Stellar". The idea was to celebrate the company because it was the best at what it did.[20] The call had the potential to take someone down to a positive level emotionally. If they realize they are dealing with someone who has a positive attitude on the phone they might re-think what they are going to say.

---

[19] Who else volunteers their spare time renting cars to paying customers?
[20] It was most certainly not the best car rental company out there.

This carried over well especially into my next job working for a supplier of sealants and glazing materials. Grouchy old contractors were taken back by the person answering the line, and they usually responded positively.

I knew I was not going to last long or become a "Stellar" employee of "Stellar" car and truck rental. Calgary had a busy market for work and I knew there was going to be something better that paid better. Just before I was able to leave the job I endured a brutal evening of work with a colleague that made me grateful that I was quickly about to move on.

It was around the beginning of the Calgary Stampede. The "greatest outdoor show on earth"[21] was set to welcome several hundred thousand visitors as it does every year. We were completely sold out of vehicles.

Well, according to the call center in Toronto, we were never sold out. As the afternoon concluded and evening dawned, we started to get more calls from the airport's courtesy phone to pick up customers.

I panicked. We had no cars despite showing bookings. Somehow during the morning review of reservations, the branch manager missed the fact that we had several

---

[21] Given my stance on animal rights now, Stampede really needs to change or be scrapped altogether.

more bookings to honour but no vehicles to give them. Toronto agents kept booking people in without even realizing we were sold out for months. They ignored the availability completely. I turned to my more experienced colleague wondering how the hell we were going to survive the evening. No cars, and we did not want to pick people up to have them only be stranded at the branch.

"Lock it up!"

I was not sure he was serious.

"You mean close?"

"Yep. Now get the gate!" he shouted.

With still a few hours to go on our shift, we backed the courtesy shuttle into the empty back lot. My colleague hit the lights and encouraged me towards the door. It was Toronto's fault that we were overbooked. So given that the call center was a 24/7 operation, the branch calls were forwarded to them. They caused the problem so it was going to be theirs to solve.

I was happy to head home early. The day after that evening no one ever brought it up. It was as if nothing happened in the first place. No discussion among any of us in the office. A few weeks later I went to my next job still wondering about the people who were stuck at the airport.

Hope the call center staff had fun admitting their mistake and figuring out what to do with stranded travelers.

Hitting The Hills

School, supper, golf, Hit head against wall, vent frustration.

Come home, go to bed.

Get up having barely slept.

Do it all over again.

This was a regular schedule. It went on and on for a few full golf seasons.

At times, it was exhausting.

It was just as much a mental workout as it was a physical one. The centuries-old Pictou Golf course was a nine-hole course that felt like five given how close together many of the fairways were. Forget ever using a Stairmaster for a workout. You could walk this course and be more worn out from the hills in a shorter amount of time.

My brother and I both had sets of junior-sized clubs. They were easy to find at used sports equipment stores. When Dad realized we both took to the game he seized on the opportunity to get us all out many nights during the week. For the first little while Mom also came with us for some of those rounds. It quickly dropped down to the three of us. I'm sure we all drove Mom crazy after a little while of this. I don't blame her and used to think maybe I should have quit at the same time.

When Dad was off for a regular stretch of days, he would prep supper so it was ready when we walked in the door. Minutes after eating we were out the door and on the way. On arriving and signing in at the club we all grabbed whatever snacks we wanted to take with us on the course. A few cans of soda and a bag of chips then off we went.

As I mentioned a few lines back, one of the biggest problems with this old course was how close in proximity the fairways were to each other. On one part of it, holes four, five, and seven literally ran alongside each other in an open space. On a busy weekend it was common to have golfers hitting across each other. Shouts of FORE! rang out constantly. At times there would be a chorus of FORES. Even people on the farthest ends of the place would duck and cover thinking they were going to get cracked in the head by a wayward ball.

Dad and brother were in my view very competent golfers. To this day I believe my brother can hit a ball smoother than anyone. That includes several professionals that I watched and worked with during a memorable summer at the world famous Kananaskis Alberta courses.

Those golf evenings were great workouts. Because the course was so hilly, you would want to drop to the grass with exhaustion after playing one or two holes. Some of those September evenings brought out some amazing scenery. To be standing out in the middle of a fairway and look out over the harbor was like watching a constantly moving painting. You saw the shoreline, the boats, the trees and their changing colours. Some of those rounds in Pictou proved difficult physically before you even hit a drive on the course. If the wind was blowing a certain way, we had to contend with the vile air pollution coming from the nearby pulp mill.[22] Walking those hills was hard enough on the lungs. We had to breath in this toxic air if we wanted to be there golfing.

Eventually the golf evenings wore out. I started going much less. Part of it for me was dealing with arguments between brother and the old man. Part of it was boredom and maybe post-school day mental exhaustion. I started to quit halfway between rounds and wait for them in the car. Other nights I elected to stay home, read, play video games, crank music or be outside playing basketball.

---

[22] The mill I reference was the controversial Northern Pulp Mill.

During summer months was when golf expeditions continued for me the odd time. Even after my parents' divorce, Dad loved to go play a few rounds at courses in Prince Edward Island. I enjoyed those rounds even more than golfing at home. It was somewhere different. These courses were more modern compared to the home course.

The island is well-known for being a premiere golf destination. In my younger days there were a few courses where tee times were high in demand despite the low prices. For many summers we vacationed near Cavendish National Park.

The "Dish" and nearby communities have some excellent golf carved out against the backdrop of splendid natural scenery. A short golf cart drive away from the famous Green Gables Course is where you will find a great location called Forest Hills. The location is prime and the prices perfect. It was the first nine-hole course that gave us an opportunity to do something different beyond the hills at Pictou. Number four in particular was a ninety yard shot off the tee over some water[23] to the green. Skilled golfers could get this done with a pitching wedge. So before my teenage years even started, I was bragging to other young golfers

---

[23] We might as well have called it a large puddle.

about making the green in one on a course none of them had been to.

Along the scenic Nova Scotia Sunrise Trail, Dad found another course that would become a favourite for him. The nine-hole course at Brule Point[24] was another fine bit of scenery along the Northumberland Strait. It was another location to play a quick nine and be home within a reasonable period of time. Best part of this course was the lack of slopes compared to Pictou. At the end of nine holes, it was easy to still be functioning. Like the backdrop of Pictou, you felt like part of a constantly moving portrait.

The difference is with Brule Point, the ocean was constantly part of the background in those paintings.

This might be why I have a slight fascination with works of art connected to golf. I think of the times that we were out and what a great collection of pictures those all would have been. They are great in memory and would be just as amazing in photo albums or frames.

Golf is fun and occasionally frustrating. Dad told me when I was younger that it would be a game to take well into senior years.

---

[24] See "Truckin" and re-read the story about the speeder who rode the back of the truck, then was caught after we let her pass. Go on…I'll wait.

Those were among the wisest of his words.

Live From The Basement!

Some of the best times I've ever been in a band situation involved not being on stage. The best times were during rehearsals and jam sessions. It was about having a good time and for my parents, me staying out of trouble. A majority of those sessions were taped. You wanted to capture any magic that could be turned into a "hit heavy metal song". I wished all of those tapes lived today.

Thankfully one of my friends had the sharpness about him to convert a few minutes of the most memorable session to digital format. Saved to my phone and email, I have a few minutes of what we still refer to as "Live From The Basement" recorded in November of 1994. Chad is the drummer who rounded out the rhythm section we created for that early band. To this day he remains one of my favourite drummers and people in the world. When he first sat down to play behind a kit, it was as if he was already drumming for decades. He practiced prolifically using practice pads and a few sets of drumsticks. He played along to songs every single day for hours. This helped him develop an incredible sense of timing when the time came to start beating the hell out of an actual set of drums.

The great guitar player we jammed with was a bloke called J. He lived at his grandparents' place where we jammed a few times. On the day we recorded "Live", it would be downright comical. We left that day with abdominal pain and bloodshot red eyes from crying with laughter.

As musicians in a heavy rock or metal situation know, a power trio has to be powerful to get a good sound across. As a bass player, I always enjoy the challenge of filling out the extra spaces. It's fun to make sense of the sounds and figure out what goes well with it by adding extra things with the bass. With the three of us cranking it out we amply carried the volume required. I still did not have my own bass the day "Live" was recorded. My skills were developed using the first four strings of my electric guitar. I walked around playing air bass to all the tunes in my portable tape player. When I showed up at jams, it was easy to pick up and play whatever bass was nearby.

A local bloke had a great beater bass[25] that he kindly loaned out to me a few times.

---

[25] This refers to an old instrument that showed tons of wear.

Instead of needing to borrow an amplifier, I just plugged in to this ancient Sears box J had. It still rattled the foundations of the townhouse that J and his grandparents lived in. Both of us were running the guitar and bass into this same ancient amp.

The end result of that day's jam was a brash, loud collection of grindcore metal music. My parents called it noise. To us it was everything and anything. A few bars of songs we knew all the way through. A few bars of songs that were yet to be invented. My bass solo was just me running lines through a distortion pedal trying to sound like Metallica's Cliff Burton. Burton was the late great bass legend who appeared on the best albums the band ever recorded.[26]

The most memorable thing from this jam session was our tribute to a Scandinavian black metal band called Beherit. The band released an album that sounded akin to a car being slowly dismantled with a chain saw. We all screamed our best possible black metal singing voices. It sounded hilarious on tape. Of the few minutes of tape that Chad and I managed to digitize, I'm grateful some of those minutes contain our tribute to Beherit. That tribute has a permanent place on my Smartphone and home computer. It

---

[26] "Master of Puppets" is a masterwork and in my opinion Metallica's finest record.

may be the only audio file I need to keep backing up for a very long time to ensure its' longevity.

Towards the end of our recording we wrote and recorded a short song called "8.3". The piece is the three of us repeating "8.3." multiple times then screaming into the microphones. It had a single-chord structure that was repeated throughout the whole song.

It should have been a hit somewhere.[27]

When we wrapped up and did our first listen back we spent an hour afterwards in hysterics. We then went through a handful of cover songs putting our own twists and turns on Black Sabbath, Danzig and other heavy favourites. During our improvised bits, we would hear little nuances of sound that were amazing or funny. A great instrumental part could come through and we would point it out. A scream translated into a nonsensical word or farm animal. "Hey! That sounds like you are a cow fed up with the line at the DMV!"

There will never be another moment like "Live From The Basement". Chad and I admittedly tried to recreate the magic that came from that session. We ended up recording a long-gone bass, drums and vocal session at his parents place a few years

---

[27] It's understandable that it was not.

later. We lined up a bunch of crazy effects so the bass would make some odd sounds, we wrote some weird poems to read out on the spot, and like "Live" we laughed ourselves stupid.

Our esteemed trio found ourselves in a reunion back in the early 2000's. At the time, I was living in Calgary and did not get home too often. On this particular trip I was able to catch up with Chad. He had been continuing in a different band with J on guitar, and two blokes named Howie and Shane on bass and guitar respectively. They were very polished and really delivered the goods. By virtue of good timing, the chaps were to rehearse in a barn on Shane's parents property located outside of town. I ended up giving Chad a drive there since I had a rental car for the time I was home.

We were joined by another mutual friend, Hatfield. Hatfield was briefly a former neighbor of mine in New Glasgow, but we all went far back to our early teens as acquaintances.

This barn they were going to rehearse in was going to be a tight squeeze. It was very damp and rainy out and there were drafts coming in everywhere. Hatfield and I sat on the top of a deep freezer behind the drums. He broke out a large bag of weed and a pipe, and we kept trading hits off of it. Partway through the rehearsal, I started singing along to the music. Much of what they were playing was death metal covers. Most of the material on their set list was familiar to me.

For those of you unfamiliar with death metal, the vocal delivery is more growling, screaming and grunting versus actual singing. It's better to look at it as vocalizing since contrary to popular opinion, it actually requires talent to pull it off well. Shane was great at doing it. He had difficulty keeping his composure as I started lip-synching the words in perfect time while looking like I was a stoned orchestra conductor.

During a break, Howie and Shane stepped away from their instruments so I picked up the nearby bass. Chad, J and I looked at each other and froze for a few seconds. It was as if we were back in the basement reflecting on the memory.

The various music adventures we all took in younger years were many. Chad and J took things much further by working live in town. They both ended up working various gigs over the years. One thing Chad and I never did to this day was work a gig in front of an audience. Still in our middle-ages now and when we reach old age later, there will be no other drummer on earth I would rather jam with.

Confirmation Classes

How I loathed, every, second, of it.

I sat in one of the front rows at church listening to the alleged truths about a confusing book I spent two years reading.[28]

It was confirmation classes through the Anglican Church. At this youthful age, I believed in all the scientifically unproven things that church was teaching. I read the New Testament to try to make sense of it, and also because I was told reading it would bring good fortunes. Good fortune in high marks, and good fortune with girls. On reflection, I was really daft to think that reading this book was somehow a gateway to better understanding the human condition.[29] It left me further confused.

I was starting to question things. I started to read more. I was questioning why we needed to be at a ceremony to go through these motions to confirm acceptance to the church. Why was our attendance all through our younger days not enough? By attending

---

[28] The New Testament

[29] It works for some apparently.

these classes and getting a passing grade from a bishop, we would then be permitted to have a sip of cheap wine on a Sunday from a cup that was a breeding ground for germs.[30] I often wished I had started to question things like that more. I really felt like I was dragged there. In retrospect, I definitely was. I was angry that even though I considered myself a Christian at the time, it was required of me to be part of a stupid few classes then a silly ritual granting us extra-special status in church. The status granted us wine and a piece of "bread" that tasted like a shaving of soap.

During the evening of the confirmation ceremony, I remember dressing up in an ugly suit combo that was either a size too large or too small for my awkward frame. I remember Mom taking photos. Dad came to the service with a camera of his own while my grandparents attended to "renew their confirmations". That was particularly painful to watch given my Grandmother's mobility was diminished at that time. She was in pain and should have been resting at home.

It was a long, drawn out and dreary waste of an evening. No matter how nice the bishop and the reverend were as people, I was ready to snap. The bishop belonged on

---

[30] During editing of this book, we are in the midst of the COVID-19 pandemic.

a chess board. I sat with a cousin singing a famous line from Black Sabbath's "N.I.B."[31], hoping to get a few parishioners riled up.

"My name is Lucifer, please take my hand."

It did not work. Those within earshot ignored us completely. Although they probably thought we were completely mad. So I went through the motions. I became confirmed and was permitted a sip of wine on the odd Sunday that I was in church. One of the main things that I feel religion teaches is all-out paralyzing fear. To assume faith is the answer when there is no other possible solution, goes against reality and goes against science.

When I wanted to question "faith", I should have done it. I should have challenged that fear and faced it head on. The excuses my Dad and others made for religion still come back to haunt me. If I spoke up when I did, it might have led me to question things sooner. During difficult periods of my life, I leaned on religion thinking it was the answer to my calls for help. It became a crutch with no answers. Any time I made it through

---

[31] N.I.B. was actually about drummer Bill Ward's beard. It looked like a pen nib. According to bassist Geezer Butler, "the song was about the devil falling in love and totally changing, becoming a good person." (Quoted from The Black Sabbath Story Volume 1).

something, it`s because I worked my ass off to get above the waves crashing down on me. Learning to ask for help is something to be learned, and re-learned if needed.

Religion has done more to divide and conquer.[32] It still works on dividing society. Many religions work against the rights of women and minorities. They work on brainwashing people into not being able to think for themselves. It works at making people live in fear. Creationism as an integral part of many religions works very hard against proven science.[33]

Religion needs a confirmation class on *reality*.

---

[32] I do acknowledge that it has indeed helped some to escape otherwise dangerous paths. It also has provided a positive sense of community for many.
[33] We especially see this in 2020 with COVID related deaths. People think their faith can protect them from any illness.

Mrs. Shopper

Nan knew a bargain.

Unfortunately, Mom's Mom was a hoarder. When we discussed it in more detail she called it "organized accumulation". The best thing about her accumulated stuff was that there was a lot for her to give out when she felt generous. I could have walked into her place any time and mentioned something in the sweets department; chances are she had it on a shelf. Remember freeze-dried instant tea? She had it long after it was off the shelves.

My earliest memories of my Mom's parents were these shelves full of non-perishable food. When Pops passed away in 1987 we were spending more time with her. When we would pull into the driveway to pick her up and ask where we were going, the answer was usually; "We are taking Nan shopping."

I wanted to jump from a moving car so many times. It might have meant going through the window, then the nearby steep cross-streets in the town. It was nothing personal. I just loathed shopping despite learning a thing or two while it was happening. At a young age, I learned a good deal was a good deal whether you needed a particular item or not. For a time, I believed if a sale was good you should take part in it. You never know when you might need a thing or one of them deweys[34] or dealios[35] used for different things.

The idea of shopping in a giant department store for several hours was frightening. When Sears was still open they had some stores that were gargantuan. In my youth, the location at the Halifax Shopping Centre was this monstrosity of scattered things. The basement was a tornado of bins, racks and people's hands going through them. Any item you bought from the bargain basement guaranteed to come with at least a half inch of dust. Dead skin cells with a new purse? Sounds like a great deal! Put that on your stupid Sears card and pay it back later! Quality Kenmore brand dust guaranteed!

Whenever I would bring up Nan's shopping it stuck with my oldest friend how amusing my frustration was. One of us came up with the idea to call her Mrs. Shopper. It was a fair description. Within a short period

---

[34] Nan's word for anything and everything.
[35] My word for anything and everything. I heard it from punk rock bassist Mike Watt.

most of my friends knew Nan as Mrs. Shopper.

When she moved out of her house in the late-1980's she first rented this really large duplex house on the east-side of town. It was very large and spacious. More space than she actually needed. During the first month she was there, I recall wandering up a set of stairs that led to this very open top floor room. I found half a dozen bottles of bleach that were quite old. The labels were sun-bleached and sticking to the bottles.

On one of the trips we did make to downtown Halifax, Nan and I did something different to pass the time other than shopping. Brother and Mom went out on a harbour tour sailing on the famous Bluenose II. I wasn't keen on going and neither was Nan. We were at some food court pizza joint that was in one of the ferry terminals at the time. We were waiting for this boat tour to finish and had nowhere to go. At the time it cost 10 cents to cross the harbor by ferry. The weather was decent that day. So we decided to cross the harbour as many times as we could until Mom and Brother returned. We would talk about that day right up until the weeks before she passed. It remains my favourite memory of her.

Going shopping with Nan tested what little shopping patience I had as a kid. Some of that patience testing has spilled over into adulthood. There are many reasons I enjoy online shopping more. In my education as a shopper though, I've learned that certain things should be bought in person. I was in no rush to sign up for having someone pick out my produce for me.[36] I remember grocery delivery being introduced when I lived in Calgary during the early 2000's. Really it is not exactly new though. People used to call into markets all the time and place orders for delivery. Online ordering is a modern version of ordering by phone and mail.

    As crazy as shopping with Nan was, I would gladly go shopping with her one more time if just to have her still be around.

---

[36] That has changed with the COVID19 Pandemic.

A Fast 3-Count

My oldest friend is a class chap. We have known each other since the first day of kindergarten. If I were to describe Murdock I would start by saying he was a big kid. I would say now he is a man with a big heart. There is not a month that goes by where I don't think about something funny he did or said. He threw some of the best parties when we were young. He was protective of many of us. One day when I was on the receiving end of taunts and closed fists, he promptly threw one of the bullies into a snow bank then dropped his entire weight on top of him.

That was the end of the taunting for a very long time.

A few years later while we were in junior high, I took things a bit too far with him. We were at Chad`s[37] place partying over birthday celebrations. Chad had his room in the basement of his parents' house. We always had loud music going at all times. At any

---

[37] Same Chad from "Live From The Basement".

given moment, we would start a mosh pit in this small room. As part of that moshing we would practice "stage dives" right on to the bed. Murdock was very strong for his age and bigger than all of us. At one point he stage dove on to the bed, breaking the bed frame cleanly in half. It was a weak old frame to begin with. Of course we all found this hilarious. That included Murdock.

Sometime shortly after this we were all throwing each other off the walls and things were getting a bit heated. During a break in between songs, Murdock removed his shirt to cool off. For some stupid reason, I thought it was an appropriate time to take a dig at his chest size.

"Murdock, you should start wearing a bra!"

Everyone was falling on the floor laughing. That is, everyone except for Murdock. Within seconds he had grabbed me by the throat and side of my jeans and was pressing me up against the ceiling. He held me up there for a good three seconds before letting me crash down to the floor. It was a mirror image of a classic professional wrestling move called the gorilla press.

Thankfully, I was able to break my fall against the floor where I joined my friends in uproarious laughter. Murdock helped me back up and the mosh pit continued.

On The Eve of Examinations

High school was about survival. For me it came down to survival of the mathematically fittest. I never feared the other subjects much. Recovering from a failed mid-term exam in the sciences or social studies was easy. English was rarely if ever a problem at all. Math was my biggest fear. That fear morphed into some kind of psychotic demon starting in third grade. This was when I started to struggle and become absolutely terrified of the subject.

My teachers identified math as a weakness in that third grade year thanks to some poorly chosen words home to my parents. Because my brother is so great at it, I felt like my struggle was viewed as more of a major problem than it should have been. The extra pressure I was facing from some educators and at home was not helpful. I remember at the end of the third grade year feeling so certain that I was going to be failed out just on my math ability alone. There was no reason for me to fear anything. Teachers did not call my parents to say I was being held back. The homework struggles throughout that year were painful. I lived academically in the shadow of my brother who sailed through school with straight A's in everything. My parents incorrectly assumed that the subject should just as easily come to me. My strong subjects were not given as much attention and recognition as my weaker ones.

Upon entering seventh grade I was met with a more terrifying challenge in math class. My teacher would call us all up multiple times per week to the chalkboard to write out the answers to homework questions. I spent the longest up at the board fearing sudden nausea and perspiration equal to lengthy sweats in a sauna. Within seconds I would be the last person left at the front of the room. The comments would start from the audience. "Stupid" and "dumb" were just some of the adjectives used to describe my numerical processing abilities.

By the time I landed back at my desk after writing out the wrong answer a few times, I could have collapsed from the exhaustion of the public humiliation. I truly dreaded the days when we had to endure double periods of math. That was a form of long-scheduled psychological torture.

What saved me in seventh grade was the patience of my Aunt Shelly. She not only tutored me patiently through to a passing grade, she put up with all of my complaining throughout the whole process. Frequently I would switch subjects with her mid-session to talk music or my teenage frustrations with life. She patiently guided me back to the grind and I was able to pass the year.[38]

At the beginning of ninth grade I was moved to an adjusted learning program with a smaller class size and anywhere from one to two teachers in the class at any given time. My health was a major mess that year mentally, so having the help was beneficial. To this day I think nothing but the highest thoughts of those two teachers, Mrs. Hussher and Mrs. Bowden. They had a bigger impact and were not told enough by any of us. We should have thanked them more.

Before going into senior high school, I remember the note Mrs. Hussher wrote on my final report card of the year. "General math is recommended". General math in senior high school was the basic subject level. Halfway through the year I remember an argument with my Dad about the level of math I was going to take in senior high. Pre-

---

[38] I believe her guidance also helped me through eighth grade math as it was more of a continuation of the year before.

calculus was not an option and I felt even taking what they called "academic" would be just as worse. My brother was in grade eleven pre-cal and doing well as normal. I remember one night telling the old man that I would not be taking pre-cal. "Yes you are taking pre-cal", he replied. My memory is a bit faded after those words. It resulted in the usual escalation of voice volumes and arguments that he and I partook in regularly.

Back to that final report card and Mrs. Hussher's note. Her writing that on the report gave me a sense of empowerment. At the time my mind was made up about not going to university. It was either trade school or straight into the workforce. I took that note to my parents and said I was taking general math and that was all that would be said about it. Dad kept saying I was "making a big mistake". Given how much I struggled with even general math through senior high school, it was definitely the right call.

For reasons I'm sure made sense at the time, we needed at least two senior high math credits in order to graduate. So in theory, I could stop math after passing tenth and eleventh grade. I barely made it out of both of them and went into twelfth grade general math out of necessity. By then I needed to make the bare minimum of credits in general just to graduate high school. So on strictly the basis of numbers I had to enroll in grade twelve general math. There was no other way for me to fill my course schedule for that year. Forget the horrors of the chalkboard nightmares in seventh grade. Just sitting in that grade twelve class was difficult enough. In a class where everyone struggled to get through a day of school without feeling emotionally drained, I just did not want to be there.

Another math-related point of contention between me and the old man was the fact that you could carry a calculator in this class. "You need to use your calculator", Mr. Atwood would say. Having the push-button problem-solver did not mean we had all the answers. It was supposed to help us understand where we get to the set up of an equation. We still had to figure out answers on our own.

We reached the halfway point of the final year of school and it was the usual mid-term fear of making to the point with a failing grade. Come that time my marks landed somewhere in the high thirties or low forties. Other subjects were manageable high fifties. My English marks remained in the high sixties and low seventies. Even though I took general-level English all through senior high-school, we were mixed in with academic level English classes in the final year. So we were stuck in the same class with all the jocks and preppy snobs that looked down on those of us taking general courses.

The mid-year panic really did start to set in after getting that set of marks back. I needed to leave school with a minimum level of credits in order to graduate. If I was going to fail out, it would be because of the lousy math class I never needed to complete in the first place.

I needed serious help. I started through the year with help from a tutor who lived in my old apartment building. He cannot be faulted for my failing grade. My struggles were my own. My learning abilities were a day-to-day battle with myself. Dad found additional help from another tutor who lived a short walk from my place in town.[39] As the rest of the year unfolded I slowly managed to recover. That recovery was driven mostly by the fear of having to repeat a year of high school. The very notion of having to spend one more year in the place was terrifying. I wanted my freedom. I wanted to move on. School needed to be over and done with.

The final day of classes before exams was traditionally the record setting day for high absenteeism. People stayed home to "study". As much as I loathed being in school I showed up that day, desperate to find a way to get through it all. Homeroom

---

[39] I'm grateful he finally saw that I really needed help.

was a scattering of students at different skill levels. A few A-level achievers mixed with me and two or three others from the "rough" crowd.

I was terrified of failing the year. I needed to complete a passing mark on every course. Being a returning student was not going to be an option. I was there that day to pull out all the stops. My presence was to show that I could make an honest effort in order for the warden to let me out of the prison of high school.

Math class rolled along just before the lunch break. I walked into the room as the only person to show up. My first thought was if Mr. Atwood was going to send me on my way to study somewhere outside the classroom. To my surprise, he calmly pulled up a chair beside my desk and said "let's work on some things".[40]

He pulled several example questions from the textbook. Mr. Atwood patiently kept my focus on solving questions completely. The goal was not to rush through anything. We kept going for the whole duration of class time. It may have been the hardest I've ever worked during any class in my entire school life.

During the final exam, I kept my calm and cool. Everything I could have done, I was

---

[40] I will never forget that day.

doing. The whole morning was spent going through the pages getting every possible answer down with no detail missed. I left that exam feeling confident that I would make it. There were only one or two more exams left to go. The very last one was for Global History.

It was a glorious sunny day.[41] It was set on the calendar as my final day of school. Having survived math confidently, graduation was close in sight. Global History was taught by one the best educators I ever had. Mr. Greene had been my social studies teacher in seventh and ninth grades. As much as I loathed school, it was an honour to land back in one of his classes for the final year of my school prison sentence.

The room had about twenty students scattered throughout.[42] The monitor for the room happened to be a long-time friend of the family who was a resource teacher. She was good at keeping us trouble makers to a minimum level of disruption. It helped that in addition to being very kind, she was a black-belt in karate and no one really want to piss her off.

---

[41] I will ESPECIALLY, never forget that day!
[42] Now that I think about it, this is an early example of "physical distancing" so I'm now a pioneer or something.

I breezed through the exam much to the annoyance of Mr. Greene. It was the final day of school. Here I was unable to contain how happy I was to be released from jail. During his first round of checks into the room, Mr. Greene made a point to loudly ask that I not rush through the exam. "Check your work, use the time wisely". As much as I respected him, all I heard was "*blah blah blah*". Still, I knew we were going to have to remain in the room until a certain time on the clock before we could be let go.

On the very last question, I left my final answering sentence open without closing off punctuation. When Mr. Greene made his final round into the room, I was sitting there making two-handed stabbing motions towards the paper on my desk with my pencil. My antics were drawing audible snickering from other students. Mr. Greene walked towards me and commented on how I should go back and check everything. He suggested there was no way I could be completed the exam.

"I'm not finished. I have to put a period at the end of this sentence". Mr. Greene tried to contain a chuckle. The room monitor could not, neither could the other students. I resumed my stabbing motion towards the paper feeling anxious about getting out of the building at the earliest opportunity.

A short time later I completed that sentence. Finally, the room monitor had enough of my nonsense. She shook her head and let me leave. My sprint for the car would have matched or broken some Olympic records. My highway speed back towards town was more suited for the raceways and a hefty fine from traffic police.

On the stereo blared Alice Cooper's "School's Out". I had the tape ready from the night before. School was out.

Finally, school was out, forever.

When the final report cards came down, my subjects were all passes. The math mark landed squarely on fifty. I just made it out. To this day I do not know if I actually passed the exam enough to make the fifty. Maybe the effort resulted in Mr. Atwood pushing me over the top. Maybe he did not want to see me having to return to his class next year?

Maybe he is one of the reasons I was able to make the escape from high school prison a reality.

Unfit Fitness and Basketball

In selecting pieces for this book, Chad reminded me about one I shared related to one of my high school gym classes. It led me to thinking of another story from eighth grade that left me shaken at the time. Now, I'm really grateful it happened.

Our school carved out a room overlooking one of the two gymnasiums that would be used for a fitness center. The two gym teachers were to encourage their classes to use it.

On a particular day our physical education teacher took us down to the fitness center to demonstrate some of the equipment. Most of the class was devoted to demonstrating a squat with a barbell weight. I was terrified at the thought of even going through it. During this time I faced relentless bullying from classmates. It was a daily drill of having to put up with so much shit from a select group of goons trying to draw in the popular girls. My fear was if I were asked to try and lift this weight that I would not be able to do it properly. Maybe I would fall over like a last-place Olympic weightlifter. Hopefully my name would not be called.

After a few guys managed to lift the weight well, my name was called.

"Dann!"

I shook my head no.

After a minute of being lectured to I begrudgingly walked up to the front of the fitness center and barely managed to lift the weight. The strain on my face showed. The laughter was painful. I wanted to run out to the highway and hitchhike home in my gym clothes.

That incident stayed with me. I've vowed to do all I can in order to be fit into my wiser years. That moment of weakness became a moment of strength. Contributing to ones' good health will result in good healthy living. I went from being a scrawny thin kid to a reasonably fit human.

Basketball was an escape for me over the course of many years. During each of my junior high school years I kept a basketball with me at all times. I spent time before classes and over the lunch hours on the courts practicing.

Dad installed a backboard and net outside the garage of my grandparents place. He also put up a pole and net into the ground at the end of his driveway.

For a year or so we would use the nets sporadically. It was something new that we might have lost interest in quickly. You know kids and their short attention spans....

In sixth grade, I tried out for the grade school team. A couple of us in the class were genuinely interested in the sport and wanted to work hard at it. Others were pushed into trying out so they would be kept busy doing things other than causing trouble. Then there were the couple of kids who were in the early days of prep to become sports jocks once junior high school would start.

I was one of the last to be cut. There were obvious reasons for the coach to want to cut me. I understand them now. I had taken an interest in shooting long distance shots. My focus on basic fundamentals was way off track. My running was fine and there were some good things that probably kept me in line to make the team. It was not enough at the end.

Never will I forget a conversation that would take place one week after two kids who made the team were gone. One had moved out of town, and the other was tragically killed in a car accident. The school principal that was also the coach took me and another kid aside to ask us if we would consider joining the team. I remember who that kid was and as excited as we were, we did not lose sight of the fact that one of those kids should be here and should be on the team.

As soon as some of the other team members found out we were now teammates, the taunting began. So I practiced harder. I worked day, night and during noon hours when we could access the gym. Sometimes that was without permission of the gym teacher. So there were lots of fist fights between chaps who at those pick-up games.

We wore these horrible old uniforms with the school dolphin mascot on them. I was wise to switch out the shorts into a pair of my own that were more comfortable and longer. The uniform shorts left nothing to the imagination. This was made more evident by the comments from the female cheering sections that were in attendance to support the popular boys on the team.

The very first game was a nice win. Everyone played well and some points were scored by almost everyone.

Everyone except me. I was sick with some cold and didn't make the game. I had been out of school the day before. This was a Saturday morning game in town. I was happy for the team but wished I could have been part of it. The next game was going to be at our school against a powerful squad with many passionate players. Some of that club's kids went on to have good high school athletic careers. They also enjoyed a significant height advantage over all of us.

That game was the worst I would ever be part of. This was a pile of sports shit. We collectively managed less than ten points. The only time throughout the game where I managed a possession, I scored a field goal from just beneath the bucket.

At least I went 100% in my shooting statistics....

Going into junior high school I was determined to try out for the team. These tryouts were much more involved. Thereced to do something well. During one of the very first scrimmages I made a long three-pointer. Throughout tryouts, I hoped my shooting abilities would gain me some traction with the coach.[43]

I would be among the last to be cut in seventh and eighth grade. During the scrimmages I took a ton of heat from others who were much better than me. On that final scrimmage I was determined to do something well. During one of the very first scrimmages I made a long three-pointer. Throughout tryouts, I hoped my shooting abilities would gain me some traction with the coach.[43]

I went out on that final scrimmage determined to make another one despite my misplaced enthusiasm. I knew who and what I was up against. I threw up a long ball despite being covered by several people and

---

[43] My downfall was how I ignored basic fundamentals completely. If my focus had been more on the all-around basics, my chances might have improved.

didn't connect. There were gales of laughter from most of the people there. It was not just my idiotic attempt at a long-shot while heavily guarded. My jogging pants were on completely backwards and had been the entire practice. The logo placement gave that away.

That same evening, I was called into a room with the final remaining people to be cut.

Come eighth grade, I was determined to do all I could to actually make the team. I felt I was so close the year before that maybe I could make it work. My practice was still intense. Day and night I worked outside at my Dad's place. Because the streetlight in the rural community cast a nice light over the net you could play well after dark. Even during the winter, I would work out in waist-deep snowstorms. The snow was helpful in ensuring a stray ball never bounced far.

While the tryouts were much better that year, I was again one of the final people cut. It worked out for the best. A few weeks after, my parents separated. I still spent mornings, lunch hours and evenings shooting rounds as a way to cope with everything.

In ninth grade life was changing more. I was getting back into music. I started to grow my hair long. Music never really left me completely. My interest in music was still a strong presence. Heavy metal was another coping mechanism. Heavy metal was going to keep me out of trouble.

The coach of the junior team from the last two years switched places with the senior high coach. Several players who were a grade ahead of me were starting senior high. They had such a great record the coach wanted to continue working with them into senior high. When tryouts were announced, the new coach made a point to mention that anyone who was among the final group cut from last year had an excellent chance of making this year's squad.

My mind was already made up at this point not to bother with trying out. I was spending more time doing social things and playing music. That took priority. I still shot baskets at school, both at my Dad's place and at the rec center near my Mom's apartment. My love for the game is still strong and still serves as a regular recreational escape.[44]

---

[44] In the summers before seventh and eighth grade, I was part of a summer youth league in New Glasgow. That first summer I averaged 8 points per game and finished with a Most Improved Player Award. The year after, my average was higher. So I knew I was good and practice was paying off.

Pizza Delivery

If you are reading this and were employed as a Pizza Delivery Driver in New Glasgow, Nova Scotia between the years of sometime in the past and sometime later within the same past, I might owe you an apology.

Whoever thought it was a good idea to prank people by ordering pizzas and sending them to the doors of random people must have been a genius or a complete idiot.

The very first home phone number I knew of was slightly off to that of a beloved now-gone pizza place.[45] The phone calls we used to receive from people wanting to order Alice's pizzas ranged from three of four to more than a dozen every single week. It was tiring for my parents, but they never did anything about it. As I grew older, it became a great source of amusement to me. When my folks split, my Mom took this particular phone number with her to the apartment she moved into. By this point I was in junior high school. The calls kept coming for Alice's....

---

[45] Alice's Pizza.

"Can you get a pizza ready please?"
"Sure, if I knew how to make one."
"What?"
"This isn't Alice's dude." (CLICK)

A few times I pretended to take the orders from customers. When they asked for totals, I would make numbers up out of thin air. This resulted in a few people thinking they were getting pizzas at significant discounts, or outrageous high cost.

"What do you mean fifty bucks?"

"Yeah you know, free-trade agreement, price of cheese is up…."

Other times I called in these peoples orders for them! Sometimes I would get them done up exactly as they wanted if I was feeling generous. Other orders I would deliberately screw up completely. I'm sympathetic to Alice now. She must have had to endure a few dozen people who showed up thinking they ordered pizza, or people who were getting the complete opposite of what they ordered! To Alice's family, it was me. I'm very sorry. To the people whose orders I messed up, I hope you enjoyed the sardines.

Prank pizza orders caught on quickly. We were all stupid kids with nothing better to do some nights but get cheap laughs at other people's expense. My friend Jono and I were relentlessly ruthless to neighbours of his Dad. Here's the kicker, his Dad encouraged it. He once told us that if he could figure out a way to rent a helicopter and have it drop a steady stream of earwigs down the chimney of these people, he would make it happen. With Phil and Lill, we were too careless and would eventually get caught sending pizzas to their door.

We made the stupid mistake of ordering extra-large pizzas with double anchovies. Somehow word got around and every pizza place in the county knew that it would be a goof. When another long-gone joint answered the phone and we placed the order, our ship was sunk. The person on the other end told us we needed to "get a life".

She was right. We needed to get a life.

Jasper to Truro

In November of 1999 I trekked back to Nova Scotia for a few weeks away from the mountains. I wanted to see if it was the right move heading west. If I spent enough time in the home turf I would know how soon before I wanted to return to Alberta. Plus, I wanted to travel across the country by train. Here was my chance. That April I started my journey away from Nova Scotia by train and it felt fitting to return home on the rails. A few weeks before leaving I bought the necessary tickets, booked a hotel in Toronto for the overnight stopover and figured out the bus fare to get to Jasper from Canmore.

If you look at a map of Alberta and see how far Jasper and Canmore are between each other, you'll figure out it is not long of a distance. It is actually a three hour drive. I knew I might have a long layover in Jasper before getting on the train. Since I would have plenty of time I figured I would spend the day touring the town. When I bought the bus ticket the day before I left Canmore, I realized the bus route would not take me up the highway north towards Jasper. A three hour trip was going to be a ten hour trip with an overnight journey up the highway to Edmonton from Calgary.

On the overnight journey from Calgary to Edmonton, the bus was mostly empty. In order for me to get some sleep, I stretched out on the last three seats at the back beside the washroom so I could try to rest. If you have ever seen these kinds of seats on a bus, you will get an idea of their limited space. There was just enough room to curl up and try to sleep. I kept dozing in and out. At least three times on the way up to Edmonton, I woke up by rolling off the seats and onto the floor in front of me.

(THUNK)

"Folks we are in Red Deer and will now break for coffee, if you are leaving the bus please ensure to return in fifteen minutes."

Who wanted coffee at three o'clock in the friggin morning? No one left the bus. I got back up off the floor, gave my head a shake then went back to sleep.

We rolled into Edmonton sometime after five a.m. I still had a time to wait before boarding another bus to head west. It was a more scenic ride through to Jasper. We were back into the mountains rolling through another one of the great national parks that I've come to appreciate.

Jasper is one of those places that is not over-developed like Banff. In my view, the parks belong to the animals first. The whole of nature should be respected. Jasper is a lovely town and for all the right reasons it should maintain itself as a slice of rocky mountain solitude.

After arriving in Jasper, I would have another short layover before boarding the train to start the eastbound journey. There was a restaurant across the street from the train station with a decent pub menu. After lunch I wandered for a bit then back through the station. The one piece of luggage I brought would not surface until disembarking in Truro, Nova Scotia. Over my shoulder was a good sized kitbag with what I thought was enough to get me through the week.

There is nothing quite amazing as watching the country go by while riding the rails. The train pulled through Edmonton in the early evening and I remember attending the dining car for the first or second dinner call. You slowly started to meet and get to know the others that were travelling and you learned their stories. One family in particular stood out to me right away. They were a youthful man and woman with a toddler in tow. More about them later.

For my sleeping arrangements I had elected to go with what was referred to as a "section". This is a semi-private bunk that the public freely passes through as they travel from car to car.[46] Prior trips I always had a private room but I figured this would save me some money and I should still sleep.

This was a major mistake. Throughout the five day trip I would only sleep a few hours. The section bunks were located over the wheel axles of their respective cars. So when the train would be travelling fast at night and taking corners, you would hear every single bit of metal grinding and squealing. Being on a top bunk also meant I barely had any room to angle myself up if I wanted to read or something.

Many of those nights I would wander up to the panoramic car and try to sleep there. The train pulled into Saskatoon, Saskatchewan at three in the morning that first night. So you would hear train porters helping to get passengers settled in. About two hours later I remember waking up and figuring I would not get back to sleep. I was at the first breakfast sitting right around 7. The scenery was against a sunny Saskatchewan background. With straightaway flat lands and no immediate freight traffic, this meant the train could go full on open at high speed. The sun painted bright streaks across the living skies of Saskatchewan. This is part of what Canada

---

[46] There were curtains at least.

is about to me. Large fields of golden grain, the food of life growing right before our eyes.

During either the breakfast or lunch sittings that day, the young couple with the child occupied one of the tables. I think they stood out because they were the only people with a child riding as part of the sleeper class crowd.

I spent much of my time ducking in and out of the bar car drinking beer and sodas, while enjoying the free appetizers the bar handed out. The bar car always felt like you were riding in the basement of the train given the window position and you had to step down to get into it. People played cards, read books or chatted up with others while they hoisted a few beverages.

After the crew change in Winnipeg, I remember going back to the bar car and introducing myself to the chap who had taken over for the remainder of the journey to Toronto. In standing at the bar, I remember seeing a bright piece of letter paper taped to the wall behind the bar. The letterhead was VIA Rail's bold logo so it drew my curiosity. While I cannot remember the exact wording I can summarize it.

There is a Mr. and Mrs. Last Name Here travelling with their son Alistair from Vancouver to Halifax. Please give them everything and anything they ask for. End of letter.

I was judgmental and annoyed. Why should these people get everything handed to them? Is it because they had a child? There had to be a reason. I didn't think anything more of it and probably ordered another drink.

The train departed Winnipeg and headed into a section of Northern Ontario's remote wilderness. It would be a wild overnight ride in the wind and rain. The squeals of the wheels were constant. I don't know how others in their section bunks could sleep through it. I could not put my walkman on and sleep through the music. Every turn I was getting thrashed around. I even hit the ceiling of my bunk a few times after the wheels hit some spots and twisty turns. There was no possible way I would get any sleep this night. At some point I wandered up to the panorama car at the end of the train. If I was going to be awake I might as well check out whatever scenery I could see through the rain.

It was pouring hard. The train was going top speed. Likely to make up for time lost during the day when we were held up due to a track repair. As the train would take sharp turns you felt the car turn then slingshot back to a straight line for a brief few seconds. Then another slingshot corner, then there was another. We were in the middle of somewhere nowhere Northern Ontario. I drifted in and out of sleep. Eventually, I made my way back to my bunk and thrashed around with the train turns until early sunrise.

The next morning I stepped out of the train in Sioux Lookout to just have fresh air. Just to take in some more scenery and be walking on solid ground that wasn't moving.

The day was spent cruising down towards Toronto where we pulled into Union Station later that night. This marked the next stage in the rail riding journey. Because there was no overnight train to Montreal I had to grab a hotel for the night downtown. The Strathcona Hotel at the time felt like the equivalent of staying in a quaint New York apartment building. The room had a similar look to the set of Jerry Seinfeld's apartment on his classic sitcom. It was a nice place to spend the evening and observe a cold Toronto street from my window. If I was not so damn tired from the lack of sleep across Western Canada, I would have wandered down to the nearby pub for a drink or three. I needed the comfort of a bed in a room that wasn't moving.

My connecting train to Montreal was not supposed to leave until around eleven. I was less than a block from Union Station so getting there was going to be easy. I was up and out the door early, wanting to take advantage of the day. My suitcase was checked all the way to Nova Scotia so all I was carrying was whatever was in my carry on bag. There was some time to kill before getting on the train so I wandered in to the CN Tower. Figured there was time to go up to the sky pod for a look around. Tallest building in the world at the time! Let's do this! I was going all the way to the top of the skies without being on a plane!

I went wandering into the lobby only to find out that the sky pod was closed. Time was still on my side at this point. Instead of being reasonable and thinking it through, I was stubborn. So instead of going up to one of the other levels I decided not to go up at all. My attitude was sky pod or nothing. I have not been back to the CN Tower since.

Foolish ignorance.

I was looking forward to the train ride to Montreal. The trains between and through Quebec and Ontario always look like they are gliding on air when you see them. When you are a passenger, they feel exactly the same. The scenery rolls by with little noise and few bumps on the tracks. For this part of the trip I was initially booked into the economy coach class section. In coach you and the person beside you are facing directly across at two other people. While still in Toronto I inquired at the counter if I could possibly upgrade to business class for the five hour ride. I learned it was very spacious and comfortable, and would come with a meal.

So I paid forty dollars for the upgrade. If you were lucky you would have an empty seat beside you, which I did! The business class car on these trains is the last one at the end. So a few people walked down to check out what it was like to hang out at the last car. For all the stops on that ride and the delay due to heavy line traffic, it was worth the price of the upgrade.

The train arrived in Montreal late enough to a point where the connecting train was held up waiting for many connecting passengers. This train was fuller than the one I took across Western Canada. In locating my new cramped bunk, I met the other occupants of the car. All four in our section were occupied by people. In one of the lower bunks across from me was a woman who was very sick. *Lovely, just friggin lovely.* I approached several crew members begging if I could be moved to one of the single-person private rooms. Despite the train being full, there were a few open rooms that remained vacant. A cousin of My Dad's was part of the overall crew that worked on this particular train. He was off on this run so I could not approach him for help. I had hoped name-dropping him would be of assistance. No such luck. They dismissed me as someone trying to take advantage of a situation, rightfully so. Maybe I should have asked nicely? I thought I did.

Before the train pulled out of Montreal, I ran into the chap who ran the bar car on this crew. Without my even saying anything he recognized me from my trip up in April. "You're Ross's cousin[47]", he piped up. Come on down and have a drink later once we get rolling. So there was some peace and solace to look forward to. At least I would know of one other person on this ride.

Sometime after the train rolled away from Montreal towards northern New Brunswick, I saw the young family and their kid again. So they were making the long trip from Western Canada the same as I was. Finally I caught the name of the kid in tow. He was Alistair. He was the same Alistair who was reflected on the memo behind the bar on the Western Canadian train. Somewhere into the evening they joined me in the panorama car to watch the night continue to set in. I struck up a conversation with the youthful matriarch. Her face displayed a combination of beauty and peak parental exhaustion. Part of me was still wondering why the crews were being directed to give them everything and anything they wanted. There must be a

---

[47] Ross was a first cousin of my Dad's. He was based in Moncton, NB. I don't have much memories of him other than a couple of family occasions.

reason. Were they previous customers coming back after a rough experience? It was none of my business really. Curiosity was getting the better of me.

I don't know how our talk opened up to the point of explanation. When it did, everything came out in the open. I was learning a hard lesson about being judgmental. Alistair's father had an inoperable form of brain cancer. He was doing fine now but it was not going to last. They all wanted to travel from Vancouver to Halifax by train. Despite being from Atlantic Canada originally, their home was in Fort McMurray Alberta. No doubt another maritime family lured away to Fort McMoney[48] on the promise of a brighter future.

She explained to me her husband's very slow deterioration in health. He was already beginning to forget some things. His energy levels were not what they once were. He looked healthy on the outside despite the start of this decline. I remember she told me he had anywhere from a few months to a year.

Her story was moving. They had a young kid who was going to lose his Dad. She was planning for the future and working on getting through the grief before it had a chance to magnify. She kept a positive tone throughout

---

[48] One of the many nicknames given to "Fort Mac".

our conversation. This was a strong person. What inspiring courage to keep pushing through so many struggles.

The next day I watched the family take a short walk along the tracks in Moncton, New Brunswick during the brief stopover there. We were still running late from the night before. Matriarch was keeping a close eye on her husband and son. A short time later when I met up with them in a common area, she told me her husband could wander off at any given point. His condition had worsened that bad over the course of a few weeks. That was going to be my final conversation with them. I was getting ready to jump off in Truro and surprise the hell out of my family. Most did not know I was coming home.

I hope Alistair and his Mom are having a good life wherever they ended up.

My Mom, Stepdad and Brother met up with me off the train. I decided to surprise Dad and his side of the family the next morning. After spending the night at my Mom's, I asked Brother to meet up with me the next morning and bring me down to Dad's place. Most of that side of the family was going to be away to a funeral. I figured I would time it so I would land at my grandparents and surprise my Grandmother first. She would not be going to the funeral as it was getting more difficult for her to move around. To make it even more of a surprise I drove the old man's car on my own so anyone seeing it would think it was my brother. As I pulled up to the driveway, Dad's two sisters were leaving for the funeral. I stepped out of the car and threw my arms up into the air. They were caught off guard.

Surprising Gran was a moment of comedy gold. I let myself into the house, immediately being greeted by their border collie. I could hear Gran clear from the next room, "Who the hell is that now?" upon my entering the room she burst out laughing. That was the hardest I ever heard her laugh in my life. That sound is permanently recorded in my memory. There are days I miss her laugh.

Peace and Potatoes

Prince Edward Island. I associate the smallest province in our country with peace and potatoes. Solitude and spuds. As a kid, I remember being on the Island for at least one week out of every single summer.[49] For day trips, we could cover lots of ground in a single day's journey. When I would return to Atlantic Canada whilst living away, I made a point to try and stop over for the day. My Dad's Mom was an Islander with deep family roots planted along the long-gone Island railway line. Anyone now taking that part of the Trans-Canada Trail will walk right by properties connected to Dad's Grandparents and extended relatives.

Prince Edward Island thrives primarily on an economy of agriculture and tourism. If you were to ask a majority of Canadians what they think of when Prince Edward Island comes up in discussion, the first answer is usually potatoes.

---

[49] Except maybe the summer of 1979 when I would have been a few months old.

Most of the times we spent on vacation would be close to the popular tourist destination of Cavendish. The "Home of Anne" was always bustling with tourists coming from all over the globe. Busloads of Japanese tourists show up because the Anne of Green Gables books form part of their school curriculum. No small feat for Canadian literature. Lucy Maude Montgomery used her gifts and life to create art that has reached the masses.

The Green Gables house in Cavendish was a place I would walk through once every summer. We would drive in from just outside town limits where we normally stayed and did a bunch of things in a morning or afternoon. The Green Gables house was always interesting as a building. The surrounding grounds were always nice to walk through. There are well-worn paths that lead the way out to Cavendish cemetery where people can visit the resting place of Anne's beloved creator.

When my spouse first visited PEI, I was excited to show her some of these interesting places. Pulling up to the Green Gables house after being away from it for so long, there was a sense that something was not right. It was all changed completely. Replica barns were built. There were extensive renovations in the house that robbed it of authenticity. Drywall was put in where it was once was just wall. Construction was underway for more fixtures to the land. Pristine green spaces were being taken away, to be replaced by fake barns in a misguided attempt to keep tourists on the property longer.

It's all so unnecessary. I'm vowing to never to go there again. I still recommend Cavendish as a stopping place. Just avoid the Green Gables house. It's no longer worth what it once was. It is my sincere belief that Ms. Montgomery would not have approved of the changes.

On the other side of this disappointment there was the joy of seeing a large space returned to nature. Cavendish was home to a very large amusement park called Rainbow Valley. People would spend entire days there. Between waterslides, boating, and other activities, one could never get bored.

In looking for Rainbow Valley it took a few minutes for me to realize it was gone after driving by where it was a few times. Later that day I would find out that the government bought the land from the park owner and tore the park down. It was completely restored to green space. I would never want to be in a crowded place like Rainbow Valley anyways if it still existed. It's so rare to see a place be returned to nature that it gives some glimmer of hope for a future that has become very eco-conscious.

During the summer trips there was one day always picked out for a drive up to the west end of the province to visit with extended family. Dad usually picked the day far out in advance so we could prep a bit for it. If the weather was possibly going to rain he might move the trip to that rainy day. Still, we did not actually mind those trips if it was sunny out. When we were at our various great aunts and uncles places, we spent much of that time outside.

My grandmother's sister Susie was one of my favourite people to visit. She was a kind woman who valued family and faith to the fullest. I was young when her husband Luther passed away. The first time I saw her after his passing, she was outside working away in her colourful vegetable garden. She literally never stopped going. Her old house was an amazing time stamp with a wood stove and several antique pieces of furniture.

In the final time I remember visiting her at her house, I remember going through her record collection. She was into old country and gospel mostly. Right smack in the middle of the stack, I found a mint-condition record of Black Sabbath's third album "Master of Reality". While it was obviously there by accident, my thought of her owning it sent me into tear-filled hysterics. Mid-conversation I turned to my Dad and Aunt Susie holding up the record. Dad was a bit stunned but could see where I was going with my next comment.

"Really?" I blurted out loud through chortles of laughter. The record belonged to one of my cousins and it was left behind when he moved to Vancouver.

In March of 1999 before I left for Alberta, I would see Aunt Susie for the final time. She was over for the weekend to visit my Grandmother. Both hers and my grandmother's abilities to travel were really limited at this point. It was still easier for Susie to get over if someone brought her on the ferry. Someone in the family spent the weekend overnights with them both in order to help them out with mobility and food prep if they needed it. That way it would not all be left to my Grandfather.

My tickets were already booked and my bags were long packed to get the hell out of dodge. I could not wait to leave and I remember talking to Susie about this. I spent hours that weekend listening to her and Gran talk about old times as young girls in Prince Edward Island. They would talk about all the knitting they did, adventures outdoors or the food they would prep.

When I left for the last time that weekend I knew it would be the final time I ever would see Aunt Susie. In making the rounds I said goodbye to her last. I leaned down to give her a hug, barely able to contain my tears.

As I pulled back from our embrace she gripped my hand and pulled me back closer to another embrace. She took the most serious tone I ever heard from her.

"Go make lots of money."

I nodded in agreement. The room was silent as I left. She kept her eyes on me when I left the room. No smile, nothing.

I've long come to call Charlottetown my favourite city in Canada and it remains that way today. You could put me in the middle of the Island's capital city and I can find my way around easily. Yet, I still get turned around and lost completely in downtown Halifax. In the heat of summer a weekend in Charlottetown amongst the great shops and historical attractions is a peaceful trip away. I've come to appreciate it so much more now.

There was one other little thing about the Island that we always thought was unique. Sodas still came in glass bottles. There were no cans of pop. You still would get these money back bottles at stores or straight out of the soda machines. We always thought these things were cool especially after they long stopped appearing on Nova Scotia store shelves.

In the late 2000's the government of Prince Edward Island started to bring in cans and plastic beverage containers. It was to generate up to a million dollars annually for an environmental fund.

I started to wonder if the amount of pollution has increased since then. I'll hold off on looking up the stats in the event they spoil my peaceful island reflections. At least coffee cups there are compostable! Smallest province in the country invested in the technology to decrease the amount of cups that end up in landfills! Wake up rest of Canada!

No Thanks, Just Looking

Drive-through. Drive-thru. Both spellings work according to the online language police. As soon as I had a license to drive, my friends and I hit many of them often for food and drink. Many evenings we headed out for coffee, cold sodas and junk food.

We created as much fun as we could in small-town Nova Scotia. Only a few of us were brave enough to venture out beyond the limits of the county line to cruise the streets of small town elsewhere. Most of my memories of driving around the home area are all positive. I did most of the driving for a group of us. I was slightly older that most of this small crowd I ran with. If we wanted to rip through the drive through I never had specifics on places we could not hit. If someone wanted one thing then someone wanted something else, we could go to both places.

On many evenings I was driving a carload around late just for something to actually do. Drive through the downtown, come around, and back downtown again. One side to the other, head over to the adjoining towns, then back again.

Sounds boring right? We did this multiple times. Our hometown is adjoined by many other small towns. Historic Pictou is the exception to the geography. If we wanted to go over there, we drove a few minutes along the highway or out the back roads towards the causeway, get round a roundabout then cruise in. At the time there was only a single drive-through there known for lousy coffee. Well, it's really lousy coffee now. Let's just say it is a very large national-brand that has become international. The coffee now tastes like drinking cigarette ashes mixed with boiling water.

Drive-through beverages and drive-through food were a big part of our lives at the time. So if we wanted something greasy we went and got it. One of my friends and I would be elated to find spare change under a couch or on the ground, then to go and spend it all on cheeseburgers.[50]

On one of these evenings, I was fortunate to have use of a friend's Dad's vehicle. One of the cars he had in his drive way was one of these large boat types that crossed-over between a sedan and a few inches short of a sedan. The nineties were an interesting decade for vehicles. Desperate designers

---

[50] Go back to "Junk Food Junking".

were perhaps working to try and get the last possible things in their filing cabinets out on the production lines. We picked up our academic genius friend "The Commissioner". He was so named because of his frame[51] and commanding presence. He dressed like a mafia boss, or the chief executive of a sports league.

The Commissioner was hungry and wanted me to drive somewhere specific so he could get a particular combo meal to eat. It was one of the burger joints running a promotion for a "hickory-smoked bacon burger". Eventually I caved in and went for that drive-through. He rolled down the back window to call out his order.

"I'll have a hick bacon burger"......

The remaining four of us in the car exploded into laughter. To this day when any burger joint runs a promotion with hickory-smoked something I picture The Commissioner[52] royally fucking up his food order into the drive-through microphone.

Besides picking up food orders we occasionally ordered and picked up nothing.

---

[51] I mean he was a big chap. Not obese.
[52] The Commissioner went on to serve a tour of duty in Afghanistan, and later took a job as a "Commissionaire" security guard at the hometown hospital. As of this writing, he is stationed in Western Canada. I am grateful for his service.

We would drive up and wait for someone on the other end to welcome us.

"Can I take your order?"

"No thanks, just looking…."

We would drive around to the pickup window and speed away laughing. One time an employee came flying out and tried to catch up to our vehicle as we sped out of the parking lot.

It was funny at the time but you cannot blame them. If they had caught up to us we would have been so screwed.

CAUTION! – Contains Language!

The 1980's brought several glass-shattering moments to impressionable youth. In third grade I met someone who would change my life and further ignite a love of music. He was one of the new kids who transferred to my school from one of the schools in New Glasgow. He had some tapes of albums by bands with giant big hair styles. The sounds these bands made were very loud. It was transporting to hear this kind of music. It was Heavy Metal.[53] This was music that scared parents and pissed off religious leaders.

I loved it.

This was around the time that the Parents Music Resource Center (PMRC) was wielding their whiny word weights from a committee room in Washington D.C. They advocated for the Parental Advisory stickers which were placed across album covers. In Canada we did not see those stickers right away. We did see a language warning

---

[53] Some of that Glam Metal could be classified as Hard Rock.

across the Guns N' Roses record "Appetite For Destruction". Because of that sticker, we all wanted the record. It was being played all over the radio with several great singles rocketing up the charts. Beyond those singles were a few tracks with lots of swearing.

Perfect. The perfect album to piss off a parent and speak for the aggression I felt as a kid. Even just asking for the record was going to piss them off even more. I wanted to spend allowance money on it. Dad objected and prevented me from getting it. Other kids were allowed to have it. Those kids were worshipped as being allowed to live life a bit more normal and more open than the rest of us.

Several years later with a booming music collection, I will never forget a particular Christmas when Dad returned from shopping at Wal-Mart. He had dipped into a bargain bin of cassettes where they were wrapped in three-packs and sold for ten bucks. He tossed a three-pack at my brother and me as he walked by.

One of those tapes was Appetite for Destruction. Immediately, I told Dad how great it was happy he finally wanted me to have the album after all these years. When I relayed the old story of when the album first came out, we had a joyous laugh over it.

"Oh well, you are older now".

Public Speaking In Private

My first glimpse into anxiety being a potential problem for me was in the fourth grade. As part of language arts classes, there was a two-week period where we had to work on public speaking on a favorite subject. For third grade speaking I wrote something about the Olympic sport of bobsleigh. I became a fan of bobsledding after watching it during the 1988 Calgary Olympic Games. Speaking in front of the small classes of twenty was easy. Half of us were already lined up along the chalkboard to talk anyway. No one really paid much attention. The subject was something I was really into and eager to share my thoughts on. They were only going to select one or two to speak in front of the combined classes, which was around ninety students. I was fine with not being in the top ten.

During the "finals" of those third grade speeches, one of the students actually threw up while she was presenting. Everyone laughed at her with only a few of us not finding any humour in the situation. But I believe after that incident I became more terrified of public speaking. In fourth grade I had written a speech about a "conservation group" that I no longer can support.[54]

I was terrified of having to speak in front of the combined classes that year. Fortunately, I had a teacher who was understanding and insightful into spotting potential mental health issues. She did not dismiss anxiety the way many professionals consistently did at the time. She wanted her students to thrive. So she allowed me to do the speech to her and a couple of other teachers over a quiet noon hour. I received the same kind of critique that others were getting and did fairly well overall with it.

Fifth grade presented one terrifying public speaking situation followed by an easy one. It was the opposite ends of the scale anxiety wise. One of my teachers took visible joy in frequently showing off my work as an example of what not to do. He did it to a few of us and it was really demoralizing. I felt targeted but I realized later on I was not the only one. It only poured more fuel onto the already burning fires of nervous anxiety. The worst moment of speaking was when we all were working on building makeshift weather instruments. The easiest things to build were barometers and windsocks. Strap a balloon

---

[54] I will not reveal who they are. Let's just say that killing waterfowl is not conservation.

over a jar, tape a straw to it and have the straw pointing at some kind of thermometer looking thing with numbers and you have a barometer.

The few people who thought to tie a dirty sock to a stick were the brilliant ones. They ended up with high marks. Two steps and there you have it! A windsock!

We all had to walk up to the front of the room and explain what we had built and what purpose it served. This particular week I was growing tired and terrified of this particular educator and his nonsense. I was also terrified of having to speak in front of him and the class. I was physically sick to my stomach at the thought of it. So come the Monday morning that I was supposed to present, I faked sick so I could go home. [55] One of my Aunts drove down to pick me up.

She did it again on the Tuesday, Wednesday and Thursday. Finally I was permitted to stay out of school and be home the Friday. All of the class presentations were done and I figured I was free. Maybe he would forget about me.

Come the mid-week of the week after I was out sick, I was called up to present my balloon cover barometer. The terror I felt

---

[55] Was not exactly faking illness. Once I left the school I started to feel better. Escape from prison! Day Parole!

was unreal. I had literally been crossing my fingers hoping he would not call on me for anything at all.

My voice shook while I stammered on about what I was holding and what it did. Students were laughing at me and telling me that my fingers were crossed. Meanwhile I was being berated for not speaking up or something. Looking down, I froze. Nothing I could do would make me uncross them. I wanted good luck so bad I believed any superstition. Teacher gave me further berating about how little I had to say. I remember walking back to my chair and wanting to cry. At least this stupid presentation was over and I never had to worry about it again.

Later that year come group public speaking season, we were all going to have to speak in front of the combined classes. What made speaking easier this time was a common thread among many of the topics. The Nintendo Entertainment System had exploded in popularity. So when it came time for me to speak I was among the two dozen kids who wanted to talk about Nintendo. Everyone listened because everyone was into it. That included all three of the fifth grade teachers. I was an arcade mall rat by this point. I loved video games and pinball. It gave me another escape from the stressors that were happening around me at home and in school. I could have talked Nintendo for hours on end. A couple of the other teachers used to ask a few of us for help with certain video games so we would write down our tips and tricks for them.

I cannot recall ever having to present a speech in high school. My writing was sharp enough by itself and stood out on its' own. Despite struggling throughout high school with many subjects, English started to emerge more as a strong suit. I could write essays on boring social studies topic of someone else's choosing or come up with a few words in order to bluff through an interpretation of a book we were reading. I remember reading Ayn Rand's disturbingly dystopian novella "Anthem" in twelfth grade and having to write a poem in response to it.[56] I did my best to interpret the book and transpose it to a summary. My English teacher wrote a note to me saying "this doesn't make any sense".

My response was "neither does the book". She appeared to agree with me and I was given a pass. "Anthem" remains one of the most frightening reads I've ever worked through.

---

[56] Ayn Rand's views are not something I subscribe to. I am in near complete agreement with her about religion. That is it.

During my forgettable half year of community college, I would get called upon to do a public presentation for the business communications class. By this time there was more of an understanding starting to emerge about anxiety disorders and mental health. Fortunately my communications professor was a very understanding individual. He allowed me to choose a half dozen people to present in front of versus having to talk in front of a sixty person lecture theatre. I spoke for a solid ten minutes about bass and the bass players who inspired me. I wrote up point form summaries of what I would say and dropped photos of those bass players into web pages accessible from a local web server.

It all worked out well.

Today I can present in front of people if it is on a subject I enjoy talking about. If I can get people to think, or share some insight into common interests with that audience, any anxiety gets easier to deal with. My complete comfort will always be first and foremost with the page and screen. I much enjoy writing the words you are reading.

Want To Drive?

I was on the road at fourteen. This was one of my many lucky breaks as a kid growing up in small town Nova Scotia. Yes it was illegal.

Yes I am grateful to have started out driving that early. At the time, Dad was driving a rusted out 1984 Toyota Corolla which was flying apart at the seams. On a few drives back down to his place he would pull over and ask,

"Want to drive?"

Of course I wanted to drive! It was easy to do. So I drove the remaining few kilometers home then into the driveway. Eventually Dad pulled that old car off the road. It would still start if you gave it a boost but he no longer wanted it on the road. So as a way to continue my learning he came up with the idea to still use that car for practice. I would drive that same car up and down the dirt lane beside the house. It was a great way to continue basic practice. Drive slowly down the lane, reverse to turn the car around and drive back up. We would turn the car into the far back of Dad's property so it was never actually on the main public road. That road was a bit dangerous in front of Dad's house anyways. Everyone loved bombing down the hill doing one hundred kilometers an hour.

Even with all of the practice, I still brought out a fail mark for my learning permit test, and my first road test. My genius brother actually studied government-printed manuals long before he even wrote his learner permit test. He could have passed his learner test at ten.

Like me, he had early driving practice thanks to our parents. Unlike me, he flew through all of his tests on the first go. His hard work had really paid off. I was too keen and too eager which resulted in too many mistakes come that first test time.

To this day I have never learned to drive a manual transmission and have no desire to do so. The one time I was going to learn while driving my spouse's old car turned into a disaster. I stalled and panicked to a point of letting a line of traffic form behind us. She was super patient despite my panic. There was no recovery from this kind of anxiety. The panic grew worse.

"Want to drive?" I asked, opening the car door and flying around to the passenger side for us to trade places.

Old Dust and Old Memories

It was suggested to me that I may have an allergy to dust. It turns out I did.[57] Maybe I just could not realistically live under several inches of it. Dust and dampness has a certain smell to it when crosses your nasal passages. Recently while preparing for a move it provoked memories of my Grandparents' basement. I loved the familiar dense air of Gramps's below ground basement radio workshop.

Decorated throughout were old photos of cars he'd seen and places he'd been. He kept several old radios around in various states of repair. This was in part due to his career as a radio tech for a regional airline. He loved having old radios around. There was usually one or two in every room of the house.

I enjoyed stepping into a walk-in storage closet full of various canned goods and carefully stored ground vegetables. I rarely found anything rotting in that place. Even most of the canned goods were things that

---

[57] I confirmed this in September 2020.

would be upstairs in the kitchen cabinets within weeks if not days. My impression was that Gran and Gramps wasted very little. They had to keep up with feeding all of the company that came through the door.

In between the breaths of old dust we would get smells from the kitchen coming through the vents. Fresh fries from the stove in that kitchen were something to look forward to. To this day, fries remain one of my favourite comfort foods. The difference is I don't use any deep-fry methods, and prefer whole food prep, over flash-frozen spuds in a bag.

It was fun to look through the lines of neatly stacked foods and pick what we liked and didn't like. Or we would play grocery store and pretend to build displays and put things on sale in case Gran wanted to sell them. Gran would play along and make up prices for us to "mark down".

The basement at Dad's old house for years felt like a world all its' own. Opening the doors you were descending to a place that felt bigger than the entire house. Every time you went down those stairs, it was for a different reason. You might have been heading down to a hockey game, a one lane bowling alley, a table tennis arena, or a workshop where I pretended to be a repairman working away on various made up projects throughout the shop. The first person who lived in that house ran a hair salon out of one side of the basement. So there was a counter decorated with some old bar memorabilia. My brother and I would play bartender serving up glasses of cold colas.

Dad was very cool about me taking the many spray-paint cans and decorating some of the walls in the basement. At the time of his passing, phrases such as "The Mob Rules"[58] and "Skate or Die!"[59] were still on the basement walls.

Below ground in those houses, there was history, and easy entertainment for the imagination.

---

[58] Reference to title of second Black Sabbath album with Ronnie James Dio on vocals.
[59] Reference to a skateboard culture saying, which was also the title of a popular video game.

Black & White Television Dinners

"What the hell is this?"

Not the words I should be uttering to my grandparents upon arriving at the lunch table. Rarely would I dare take that verbal step. But how the hell can they think the stuff in the pot was worth eating? Normally when we landed at their table, it was for classic plate of fries and something else actually edible.

When I think of beef stew,[60] I think of cubed bits of meat, potatoes and large uneven chunks of carrots mixed in with gravy the consistency of thick sandy mud.

Now picture this same stew as if you were watching it on a black and white television screen. This was my grandparents take on the traditional Scottish dish known as Stovies. There were other ingredients[61] in this revolting dish that gave it its' distinct made in 1901 frozen then thawed in a pot for twelve fucking hours colour. This vile,

---

[60] I've been vegan since September of 2017. Yes I like saying this.
[61] They will not be repeated here.

arterial clogging clamor of cooked garbage may be the one dish in the world I despised the most. I barely could get a bite or two in and would want to bail out from the table. I had to fake sick to avoid eating it. The stuff was awful. It was more appetizing to starve.

There were a few occasions when Dad took it upon himself to make it! He would tell us the morning of that day that he was going to make Stovies. Our protests were met with silence.

How ironic that some "non-meat"[62] versions of Stovies are referred to as *barfit*....

Barf it indeed.....

---

[62] No pieces of dead animal flesh, but loads of animal fats.

Goal Thief

I'm not one to boast, but I won the scoring title for in first year of hockey. The title was an engraved medal that I proudly wore around my neck for days afterwards.

To be fair, it was easy to win the team scoring title given my teammates. Wherever they are now I wish them well. We all need to face reality though. We sucked. We won some, lost more.

One of those goals should not have been credited to me. But it had to be credited to someone.

Some background will assist in laying this chapter out. I played my minor hockey for the town of Trenton. It was closer to the community where I spent most of my youth. In nearby New Glasgow, the programs were so full that they would have multiple A and B teams in each division out of necessity.

During a game in Westville I would be credited with a goal that I didn't really score. No one ever knew. During a breakaway towards the opposing net, both teams piled in around the crease and into the net at the same time. In between the pileup I saw the loose puck well past the goal line. Instinctively, I pulled the puck out and tapped it back across the goal line then waved my hands in the air maniacally. The game stopped and I was credited with the goal. In the lead-up to the post-goal faceoff I circled the other side of the rink in order to let out all my laughter.

"Trenton goal scored by number eleven Dann Alexander!"

I never told anyone that the goal was not mine. That scoring title was still mine for the taking. The next closest person was several goals behind me.

At The Movies

There was a time I enjoyed going to the cinema. Now I rarely go because well…people. You cannot press pause if you have to get up to run to the washroom. It's like opening the door of your home to complete strangers and saying come right in. My trips to the movies now are few and far between. People will argue the experience of the very large screens make it worthwhile. My determination of a movie is not going to be based on the size of the screen projection.

My hometown had one theatre right at the heart of downtown[63] while nearby Stellarton had another. On opening nights there would be lineups down the street and around the corners. I don't recall the first movies I went to see at either place. Where my memory is vivid though is when I would see large lineups forming for certain films.

---

[63] In 1946 The Roseland Theatre in New Glasgow became home to a notorious chapter in human rights history. Viola Desmond's story of defiance is inspiring, and she now is pictured on our ten dollar bill.

When Dirty Dancing was released, the lineups at the Roseland wound the corner, around the block and down the back streets of downtown New Glasgow. I could not believe that so many people were lining up to see a movie. Come later grade school years I started wanting to go more to shows because film would become a big part of my life. It was insight into writing and storytelling. I was in those large lineups for several hits that would be held-over for weeks because of the revenue they generated for the cinemas. Home Alone, Teenage Mutant Ninja Turtles and Dick Tracy I went back to see multiple times. Home Alone was the first movie I saw where I remember people erupting in laughter. Anyone who has seen Home Alone will remember the many classic scenes.

There was a boring school field trip to the Roseland where we saw "The Land Before Time". It is a depressing animated film that I never want to see again. I was just happy to have some time away from school. Combined with several other schools we were all lined up around the block. The only thing that was memorable about this trip was watching a large bag of popcorn go flying over the balcony edge down to the audience below. While funny, it was actually a legit accident where someone lost their grip on the bag.

The final film I saw before the multiplex opened was Star Trek VI: The Undiscovered Country. In my view, it remains a great piece of the Star Trek storyline. The cinema was packed. It was truly a great movie experience. This is one example I can say where seeing a production on the big screen made the difference. That experience vaulted Star Trek VI into my top ten favourite films of all time.

Shortly after seeing Trek VI, the Foord and Roseland closed for good. New Glasgow's multiplex opened its' doors to eagerly awaiting audiences. Multiple screens meant there were multiple shows to see during multiple times. A group of us were still going to see shows on the odd weekend.

The Forrest Gump previews were drawing people in with an ascending level of anticipation. Chad[64] and I both had girlfriends at the time and we all decided to double-date seeing this movie. By the time we went it had already been playing for a few weeks. It was moved over to the smallest theatre in the multiplex. I remember we were quite late getting to the show that night. We grabbed our tickets and rushed right in just as the previews ended. The place was

---

[64] He has returned!

packed. The four of us sat in the last available seats near the front row.

The hype lived up to our expectations. Forrest Gump deserved all the critical acclaim it received. Decades after the release we both cannot watch it without remembering our impromptu singing session in our cinema seats.

One of the many prominent songs from the Forrest Gump soundtrack is the often played classic rock staple "Sweet Home Alabama". Chad took the chorus of Lynyrd Skynyrd's signature track and rewrote it. In a low voice audible enough to myself and our girlfriends, Chad began to sing;

"Sweet fuck, I'm in trouble,"
"Came home after two,"
"Sweet fuck, I'm in trouble,"
"She didn't know I was fuckin you"

Even our girlfriends who were trying to get us to shut our gobs were snickering. We sang in perfect time as the chorus came around again. "Sweet Fuck I'm in Trouble" has become a permanent treasure. If this were to come on the radio I keep it on long enough for one rendition of the chorus.

Green Grass

When my Mom moved into her second apartment post-divorce, it would place me in the pathway close to a neighbor with a penchant for pot. By this time only a few of us in the same social circle had tried marijuana. Any time we were around it would only be wherever this chap Mick was. Mick was J's[65] cousin. He partook in bottle tokes on a nightly basis and managed to function really well. His guitar playing prowess was the envy of many in town. Few if any could come close to his mastery of metal riffing. When he ended up moving into town he was the first of us all to have an actual job.[66]

Mick was not the neighbor who would bring me my first dose of grass. One night there was a group of younger idiot kids causing trouble on our street. They were mouthing off to anyone who walked by us.

---

[65] See Live! From The Basement. The Same J.
[66] Mick was a real hard-working bloke. He hustled to find work and we all should have followed more in that path.

We did our best to ignore them, eventually chasing them off. The group of us outgunned them physically. As we were sitting outside chatting, we saw a tough-looking bloke walk up the street into the light calling out to this group of kids. He could have been heard two blocks away. An elderly resident a few houses over came out of her house and started yelling at us for causing noise. She saw us all chasing after the lot of troublemakers. She moved close to us all to say that she was calling the police to round us up.

We all tried to explain to her that we were chasing the real troublemakers and getting them away from the properties they were walking around. Including hers! She was not having any of it. Our protests turned into a name-calling contest that we were clearly winning. We waited outside because we were all going to explain to the police that we were not the bad guys despite our creative name calling.

The police never arrived.

We all shook hands with the new associate in our neighborhood. Curt was an interesting character with a quick wit and temper. A few weeks after that incident some of us were over at his place getting introduced to Ultimate Fighting Championship events. He was into it and collected the first four or five events on VHS tape. We spent a good part of the evening there watching the events. Afterwards Curt would go outside and smoke up some weed which we eventually all would take up.

Some of the music we were listening to promoted a pro-legalization message for the great green grass. We all did the reading and believed it had some sound science to it. Contrary to what the older social conservative generation believed, we were not at all brainwashed. I would say that we were brain enhanced. Quite frankly, a bit of grass might help the world relax our overactive imaginations a bit.

On a particularly bright summer afternoon Curt, Chad and I walked up to a nearby elementary school for fresh air. We lit off a large joint while hanging out on some playground equipment. The school is right in the middle of a busy residential area and a summer day camp program was in progress! We could be seen by the kids occupying the classrooms. We were all so baked rather quickly we had no fear of the cops showing up.

Sometime during that same summer we brought J outside to smoke a bag full. Our walking tour brought us over to the old Westside School. This old building had been there since the turn of the century. My Grandmother had gone to school there. One of my cousins was among the last group of kids to attend school there before it was converted to office space and a daycare.[67]

It was late at night and we were all feeling pretty light. J was a bit apprehensive when it came to weed. He was not keen on trying it despite being around clouds of the stuff in the homes of his older friends and relatives. He had several pulls off a joint and started to spaz out a bit to our delight.

We arrived at the school playground and took up seats on the swing set. Curt managed to convince J to lie down directly underneath one of the swing seats. J fashioned a headrest out of his jacket and complied willingly with Curt's direction. For whatever reason, I did not partake in as much of the grass inhaling that night.

Curt told J to look straight up and keep his eyes open. His nose was inches away from the flexible rubber of the swing seat. Curt picked up the seat and hurled it down directly to J's face. Being stoned and watching something come at you full force might not have been a great combo. It sent us into ear piercing gales of laughter that woke up a few people close by. Even J was laughing as Curt continued to scare him stupid by repeating the stunt multiple times.

---

[67] It has since been torn down and the land redeveloped into apartments.

Unfortunately, Curt ended up getting into trouble down the road resulting in custodial jail sentences. Rumour was that he was sent to work on a rehab ranch, hence earning the nickname "Neon Rider" for life.[68]

---

[68] "Neon Rider" was the name of a short-lived show based on a kind of juvenile detention center that was also a ranch.

The Cable Is Out!

Volunteer work should be rewarding and interesting. The first volunteer opportunity I was involved in was through the local cable access station just outside my hometown. The bus drove by the place so I was able to disembark there and spend an hour or two learning some things about audio/visual production.

Public access television at the time was littered with a variety of interests. Anyone could pitch a show and was guaranteed to get at least a tryout. Some of the shows were so obtuse and witless.

When requested, I would come back to volunteer in the evenings when shows were being filmed live. The local animal shelter used to run a weekly bit where they featured animals that needed to be adopted.

It was one of my first looks into the windows of animal rescue. A passionate professional would get several cats into carriers and bring them to the studio for "People and Pets". I would help work cameras or bring in animals to the presenters. More times than not, the presenter did not have names for the animals.

One memorable evening production came apart at the right moment. I was working cameras in the studio with another volunteer and some kind of audio issue came up. The director "Ron" came into the studio from the control room just as one of the unnamed cats was brought up to the presenter. Seeing Ron run into the room, the presenter smirked into the camera and improvised a description that was meant to roast Ron.

"So, this is Ron! He can be quite lazy at times and is really difficult to look at. But he really needs a loving home of his own with no roommates."

As she was continuing her roasting of Ron, Ron was scrambling behind the camera to get some microphones corrected. Both myself and the other cameraman had fallen apart. Our laughter was picked up all of the studio microphones. In the control room, two other volunteers and a production assistant were behind the board looking down in visible discomfort from laughing. Ron was trying to get their attention. As the presenter is continuing to describe Ron the cat, Ron the director is doing jumping jacks in front of the control room window trying to get the attention of the blokes behind the audio mixing board. They adjusted a level and the broadcast continued. I had to put the camera on one spot in the studio and then join everyone in the control room. I was laughing too loudly. I hope the poor cat was eventually adopted after being described so rough.

One of my first major exposures to the inner workings of politics happened in 1993 during an afternoon of work at the station. This was in the middle of a national election campaign that would see the governing Progressive Conservatives reduced to two seats across the country. When I arrived, the Liberal candidate had just wrapped up her presentation. She was getting ready to leave but made sure to stop and talk to all of us. I cannot remember what I said to her exactly. There was probably some concern about the loss of passenger rail service which affected so many communities.

The Progressive Conservative candidate and his handlers were getting ready in the studio. They were going through a list of written questions while the candidate was robotically going through the answers. One of the campaign workers was nosing in and out of the control room trying to take charge of the proceedings.

Fortunately, the other studio director was working that day. Scotty was having none of the bullshit from everyone. The PC party was desperate to make their candidate look good at any cost. It only confirmed for me that they were scraping the bottom of the pot in order to save face.[69]

When I watched the clips later on, I started to appreciate the art of watching paint dry.....

The directors at the station trusted all of us to answer the phones for them when they rang. We knew how to put calls on hold and transfer to whomever they were for. One afternoon I was having coffee with Scotty and he was monitoring some equipment. It was technology deployed to synchronize certain American network feeds into one channel. On one of the screens you would see a channel that was carrying some stupid soap opera. You know this kind of garbage. You can switch the names around to General Children or All My Hospital and people would still watch them. It appeared something went awry with the equipment because NBC was suddenly off the air. I did not understand at the moment it had nothing to do with the local cable carrier.

Within a minute of NBC going off, the phones started to ring. I answered one from a rude elderly lady complaining about why NBC was out. Placing the call on hold I

---

[69] The defeat of the governing PC Party was a spectacular loss for a party in power on the national stage.

turned to Scotty who wasn't even bothering to answer the other ringing phone lines.

"They want to know why NBC is off the air."

"Fuck em, tell them we are working on it and hang up."

So I did exactly that. We kept the phones ringing. Scotty made his point clear and I felt proud to have hung up on someone who was being rude. It was one of those moments that it dawned on me how dependent people were on television. Did she really need to know what happened that instant in her story? She could buy one of those trash rag pocketbooks at the grocery store counters a week later which would spell out what happened to Marlena's brother's cousins' father's niece's nephew....or whatever the hell bullshit story was being told.

Well, That Was Stupid!

In the summer of 2000, I was living in between Canmore and Calgary Alberta. I was slowly trading in the mountain town for what would turn out to be a disastrous roommate situation. Prior to my moving I learned one of my favourite classic rock acts would be playing a show at a popular Calgary venue.

In the years leading up to my move west, my work reviewing music had put me in contact with Blue Oyster Cult guitarist Donald "Buck" Dharma and then-time bassist Danny Miranda. Both of them class acts and great musicians. Before I moved to Alberta I had written a positive review of their recent release, "Heaven Forbid". Through that work I was able to get an interview in with Danny. The review I wrote for a long-gone online magazine was glowingly positive. In the summer of 99 I had written Buck to wish him a good summer and inquire when and if they would be coming to Calgary. Later the same day Buck wrote back to tell me they were playing Calgary the very next night. There was no way I was going to make that concert. Maybe I was scheduled to work or something. Buck had told me via email they expected to return to Western Canada again in a year.

So one year later I made sure to follow the tour schedule and get tickets for the show. By this point I owned a car and could easily get to the show. The concert was going to be at a normally packed nightclub in the heart of downtown Calgary's entertainment district. I arrived early with no set plan to return to stay with friends that night or continue back out to the mountain town. I made the conscious decision not to drink that night, although I could very well have hoisted a few. Getting there early enough to the venue gave me the chance to circulate around and just enjoy the sounds. I cannot remember who the opening act was, just that they were great.

While the opening act was on, I spotted legendary hard rock/heavy metal drummer Bobby Rondinelli[70] in the audience. I knew he was going to be there as he was playing drums for Blue Oyster Cult at the time. My introduction to him was through the Black

---

[70] Bobby's discography is a stunning look into heavy rock history. He has shared the stage with legends, and in my view holds a place with them as a legend himself.

Sabbath album from 1994 titled *Cross Purposes.*[71]

In between songs, I walked up to Bobby and introduced myself. It was a real honour to be standing there chatting to a former member of Black Sabbath. We chatted about the Sabbath record, and an upcoming project he was going to be doing. We hung out for three songs before he had to leave to get ready. He made a point to thank me for introducing myself and hoped that I would enjoy the show.

Before Blue Oyster Cult took the stage I found a couple of bar stools to sit at on the far side. So my angle looking at the stage was almost completely sideways. The great thing about that location was it would be where the band would take the stage. I was going to do my damndest to say hello to the band as they walked on without sounding annoying.

There was a lengthy intermission while the bands changed out their stage setups. I mistook one of the road crew members for BOC's other guitarist and vocalist Eric Bloom. The roadie could have passed for a twin. I ended up chatting to this roadie for a good few minutes before I realized he was not Eric Bloom. Cool as can be I acted like I knew all along. He might have thought we

---

[71] This album is from the era with vocalist Tony Martin.

met at a previous concert. As he worked on tuning instruments he shouted out to me that I could "join them all backstage afterwards for the post-show gathering".

For reasons I will never understand, I politely declined.

As the band started up to take the stage I was able to chat with Danny Miranda who was absolutely delighted to see me. Guitarist and keyboardist Allen Lanier[72] looked at me thinking I was some excitable music nerd. He calmly nodded in his cool sunglasses as he walked on stage.

It was a really great show. The audience rocked out to well-known classics and some newer material. When they played some of the newer tracks I was the only one singing along. Danny acknowledged that from the stage pointing at me in between some bass lines. During one of the solos Danny and the other bandmates were off stage giving the soloist the spotlight when he approached me to ask if I was dropping by the after party later. I declined likely out of nervousness and the fact that I might be driving later.

The show wrapped and I took a cab back to the apartment I was staying at. For some idiotic reason I elected not to park downtown. I could have just done that and spent less on

---

[72] Allen passed in 2013 and I am so happy I was able to see him play live.

the fare! It's not like I was drinking that night! The high from the show was so strong and my adrenaline was rushing. So I hit the highway back to Canmore. I was driving 140-150 kph on the quiet highway, listening to a tape of classic BOC songs that I just heard live in a concert, under a clear summer night rocky mountain sky.

I rolled in to Canmore around 1.a.m and slept for a few hours. It wasn't until I woke up that I realized. I turned down the chance to hang out with some of the greatest musicians of the hard rock genre...

Well, that was stupid. Moving on....

A few years later I was fortunate to have gained some experience jamming with many musicians in Calgary. There were several bands I was involved with as they prepared for stage shows that never ended up happening. Some of it was my own fault. There were a couple of great groups with good set lists that narrowed ever so close to live shows. Then I bailed before the shows ever happened. Much of that was my fear of not being able to survive a late night during the week.

I did what I could through music contacts to keep up my own practice as best as possible. Through those contacts I met this drummer who lived a short walk from my place. He wanted to set up a jam just in his living room for anyone to attend. There would be no other bass players so I would have that chair all to myself and could stay as long as I wanted.

"Whitey might show up so that would be cool."

"Ok great!" I replied with fake enthusiasm, not knowing who the hell Whitey was.

I was one of the last to arrive for the jam. This drummer's place was so cool and it reflected his personality somewhat. He had a pet boa constrictor whose tank that took up half the living room. It was full of heavy metal posters and music equipment scattered all over the place. In the back part of the house a jam space was set up complete with a drum set, several guitar stacks and microphones everywhere. "Whitey" had already arrived and was tuning up as I recall when someone introduced me to him.

As it turned out, "Whitey" was Whitey Kirst, guitarist with legendary punk rock icon Iggy Pop. My knowledge of him was minimal so I did not feel the pressure to play my ass off since it was about having fun anyway.

Calling that night a fun jam would be an understatement. Towards the end of the evening the number of participants dwindled down to a trio of myself, Whitey and the drummer who set this all up. Whitey led us through a list of heavy rock and metal classics. He played out a couple of Judas

Priest songs that I knew. I think he was a bit shocked that a younger musician was well-aware of the back catalog of one of metals' finest acts. So I felt confident enough to step up to the mic and belt them out on vocals. As much fun as I was having, I did not want to make it too late of a night. There was work the next morning where I was into the second week of a new position as an account manager for a trucking company.

Because this jam was just up the road from where I lived and I had really hit it off with everyone, it didn't even cross my mind to exchange contact information with everyone else that was there.

Well, that was stupid.

A few days later, I was rear-ended by a garbage truck. The car was totaled. It sent me to hospital with a myriad of soft-tissue injuries. It could have been so much worse. My music playing days were on hold. During my long recovery, anytime I picked up a bass would be when sitting down. Standing for too long was proving very difficult.

That accident ironically set me on a path towards smarter decisions. After years of job jumping I returned to college in order to make a better life for myself. Writing is my main trade, but a day job is necessary to ensure bills can be paid.[73]   Graduating college was a relief. I did not go to my high school graduation and wanted to continue the tradition. With my Mom having flown out to the ceremony though, the compromise would be to walk across the stage and then right out the door.

I left the stage diploma in hand, threw off my grad robe and left the auditorium hall.

Well, that was smart.

---

[73] I highly recommend Sara Benincasa's book "Real Artists Have Day Jobs." If you are an artist, it will leave you feeling better about yourself.

For Joe Fraser

Dad's old property had a horseshoe-styled driveway. All gravel that turned to a mud pit in the heavy rain. Lots of room for parking even if one went on to the grass. Come winter, it was a challenge to clear with just a few shovels that were never worth using. In a heavy storm it was only worth it to shovel out half of the driveway in order to back cars in and out. As soon as the plow would come by, the driveway would be filled back in. We were lucky a few winters when the plow drivers would pick the blade up in order to not dump more in the yard. We lucked out on those days because it meant that a family friend was driving the plow that day. He often spared us the extra headache of more labour.

On some mornings we would luck out extra. The community was home to a farmer with a reliable tractor. Joe Fraser would stop by the community mailbox that was at the other end of the driveway to pick up his daily delivery during the week. On the snowy days he would pull up in the truck you could see him survey the driveway to check the accumulation. If you could catch him he would call out to us that he was going to be by in a bit to "give the road a scrape". On most snowstorm days he usually did come around. He would head up the road in a reliable old tractor with a well-worn plow on the front. It would take no time to do a driveway of any size. After Joe finished with Dad's driveway, he would head up the road and take care of a few more places in the community. Just to ensure a few people could get out.

He really enjoyed doing it. Starting back to when my parents were still together, they would try to leave gifts in Joe's mailbox or take them down to his place. The gifts always ended up back in our mailbox. He never wanted a thing for any of his help. Long after my parents' divorce, Dad would still occasionally try to put gifts in the mailbox. Again to no avail. They ended up returned. Joe prevented a lot of backaches for many people. A few hours after he cleared the driveway, you would see him drive by again as he made the downhill-then-uphill trek back towards his farm.

The winter before Dad passed away, Joe had taken the season off from plowing but not by choice. Dad told me that the old tractor had broken down and it would be a while before it would be fixed. That may have been one of the few winters that Joe never made it around to shovel people out.

It was early 2014, shortly after Dad passed away suddenly when a mid-December snowfall that started the day after his funeral would fill the driveway in completely and bury an old car left behind. The house was vacant and we were awaiting better weather to prepare the property for sale. We were fortunate to have associates check on the property during this difficult time. Joe was still coming up the road and clearing just enough room for people to get to the mailbox. I certainly would not have blamed him for not clearing the driveway. Pathways were shovelled in order to get to the doorways and people were making regular enough visits. Energy-saving lights were left on so it really did sort of look like the house was still occupied by someone.

In any snow-storm, I've thought of Joe Fraser. While I don't own a tractor with a plow, I've stepped in to help people in the community with shovelling when I can. When I had a larger property, I've been fortunate to have people close by who own snow blowers. I'll offer them some fuel and they kindly will help clear up the roadway.

Joe passed away in October 2019 having only "retired" in the last few years from plowing driveways in the winter. He was a great example of how to be a great community neighbour.

Mowing With Scissors

There are many memories of Nan[74] that bring joy. The one that draws the most laughter is the day we pulled into the driveway of her old house and saw her in the yard, cutting the grass with a set of shears.

She had a perfectly working lawnmower.

---

[74] See "Mrs. Shopper"

Afterword

In compiling and editing material for this book, the world changed drastically. The COVID-19 pandemic of 2020 has proven to be a moment of reckoning for history. In difficult times like the pandemic, there is potential for greater good to emerge.

As I worked through the editing process, the theme behind this collection has become much more relevant. We are all storytellers. We cannot waste an opportunity to tell those tales.

To ensure I forget no one this time, my expressions of gratitude will be kept short.

Thanks to all of you. Thanks to family, friends, colleagues and critics. Thanks to readers past, present and future.

Let this book be a reminder that supporting the arts is an opportunity to discover the true beauty in the world.

Dann Alexander

www.ingramcontent.com/pod-product-compliance
Lightning Source LLC
Chambersburg PA
CBHW071222090426
42736CB00014B/2943